BREAKING THROUGH
THE BOUNDARIES

The American Society of Missiology Series, published in collaboration with Orbis Books, seeks to publish scholarly works of high merit and wide interest on numerous aspects of missiology—the study of Christian mission in its historical, social, and theological dimensions. Able presentations on new and creative approaches to the practice and understanding of mission will receive close attention from the ASM Series Committee.

American Society of Missiology Series, No. 59

BREAKING THROUGH THE BOUNDARIES

Biblical Perspectives on Mission from the Outside In

Paul Hertig
Young Lee Hertig
Sarita Gallagher Edwards
Robert L. Gallagher

ORBIS BOOKS
Maryknoll, New York 10545

The publishing arm of the Maryknoll Fathers and Brothers, Orbis Books seeks to explore the global dimensions of the Christian faith and mission, to invite dialogue with diverse cultures and religious traditions, and to serve the cause of reconciliation and peace. The books published reflect the views of their authors and do not represent the official position of the Maryknoll Society. To learn more, visit www.maryknollsociety.org.

Library of Congress Cataloging-in-Publication Data

Names: Hertig, Paul, 1955- author. | Hertig, Young Lee, 1954- author. |
  Gallagher, Sarita D., 1977- author. | Gallagher, Robert L., author.
Title: Breaking through the boundaries : biblical perspectives on mission from
  the outside in / Paul Hertig, Young Lee Hertig, Sarita Gallagher Edwards, and
  Robert L. Gallagher.
Description: Maryknoll, NY : Orbis, [2019] | Series: American society of missi-
  ology series ; no. 59 | Includes bibliographical references. | Summary: "The
  authors in this volume draw upon biblical narratives to highlight key roles
  played by Gentiles in the service of God's mission. Each biblical account is
  linked to a current, real-world issue as an application of the missiological
  insights gleaned from the biblical source. The biblical sources drawn upon
  include Abraham, Ruth, and Hagar; the current contexts addressed include
  Papua New Guinea, Chicago's immigrant communities, and North American
  encounters with God outside the Christian Church"— Provided by publisher.
Identifiers: LCCN 2019017387 (print) | ISBN 9781626983182 (print) | ISBN
  9781608337804
Subjects: LCSH: Righteous Gentiles in the Bible. | Gentiles in the Bible. | Mis-
  sions—Biblical teaching. | Church and social problems. | Mission of the church.
Classification: LCC BS1199.N6 H47 2019 (print) | LCC BS1199.N6 (ebook) |
  DDC 266—dc23
LC record available at https://lccn.loc.gov/2019017387
LC ebook record available at https://lccn.loc.gov/2019980408

Dedication

Paul G. Hiebert, PhD, was a student's dream for a doctoral advisor. Although he looked white on the outside, he acted more Asian. Although he was a male, he championed gender equality and equity. His love for his wife, Fran, was so dear that I (Young Lee) remember him saying how much he was looking forward to taking her honorary Doctor of Ministry diploma to heaven for her. Fran passed on before finishing her degree. The influence of his teaching and writing continues to live in *Breaking Through the Boundaries* and beyond.

Contents

Preface to the American Society of Missiology Series   xiii

Acknowledgments   xv

Introduction
Paul Hertig   xvii
    Where Do We Begin?   xxii
    Chapter Summaries   xxiv

1. **Abraham: For the Nations, from the Nations**
   Sarita Gallagher Edwards   **1**
       Abraham for the Nations   2
         Identity as a Migrant   2
         Relationships with the Nations   4
         The Nations as a Blessing to Abraham   5
         Abraham and the Nations: Outside In,
           Inside Out   7
       Abraham from the Nations   10
         Ethnic Identity   10
         National Identity   12
         Religious Identity   13
         Socio-religious Identity   17
       Conclusion   18

2. **Missional Revelation through the Story of Hagar
   the Egyptian**
   Sarita Gallagher Edwards   **21**
       Historical Background   23

Hagar as a Theologian   26
Missional Motifs in the Hagar Narrative   31
    God's Sovereignty over All Peoples   31
    God's Faithfulness to Humanity   34
    The Universal Nature of God's Mission   40
Conclusion   41

3. **Egyptian and Midianite Influences on Moses**
   Paul Hertig   **43**
   Moses and Joseph: Intercultural Parallels   43
   Baby Moses's Initial Encounter with
       Egyptians   45
   Moses Changes Sides   48
   Moses the Egyptian Becomes a Midianite   50
   The Wilderness Revelation   54
   Zipporah's Interfaith Experience with
       Moses   56
   Moses's Return to Midian (Ex 18:1–27)   60
   Jethro's Influence on Moses   61
   The Mixed Multitude and the Nations   66
   Breaking the Boundaries
       from the Outside In   67
   Contemporary Application   69

4. **Philistine Migration: Biblical Case Studies of
   Non-Israelite Migrants as God's Missionaries**
   Robert L. Gallagher   **71**
   Biblical View of Migration   72
   Missional Landscape of Samuel   75
   Obed-edom: The Keeper of the Ark   78
   Obed-edom's Family: Keepers of the Ark   80
   Cherethites and Pelethites: The Bodyguard
       of the King   81
   Loyalty in the Midst of Rebellion   84
   Ittai the Gittite: The Servant of the King   86
   Absalom's Civil War   87

Contemporary Application　　90
Conclusion　　92

5. **Naomi and Ruth: Displacement, Dislocation,
   and Redemption**
   Young Lee Hertig　　　　　　　　　　　　　　95
   Neoclassical Economic Policy and Humanitarian
   　Crisis　　96
   Crossing Multiple Boundaries (Displacement and
   　Dislocation: *Gêr* and *Nokriya*)　　98
   Intergenerational and Interethnic Solidarity
   　(Jeong)　　101
   Navigating the Patriarchy　　102
   Contemporary Application　　108

6. **Mordecai and Esther: Intercultural Negotiations
   and Power Dynamics**
   Young Lee Hertig　　　　　　　　　　　　　109
   The Drama of Power Banquets　　109
   Two Extraordinary Queens　　111
   Five Risks　　114
   　Concealed Jewish Ethnicity　　114
   　Becoming Queen　　114
   　Purim　　116
   　*Approaching the King without a
   　　Summons*　　118
   　Hosting a Series of Banquets　　119
   Contemporary Application　　120

7. **The Magi and Matthew's Approach to the
   Religions**
   Paul Hertig　　　　　　　　　　　　　　　125
   Stars and Messianic Expectation　　126
   The Origins of the Magi: Zoroastrianism　　127
   　Ahura Mazda and the Bright Star　　129
   　The Virgin Birth　　131

The Magi Are Gentiles   132
    *Wisdom Enters Judaism from Outside and
        Challenges Authority*   134
    The Balaam Connection   136
The Universal Scope of Matthew and Interreligious
    Implications   140
Contemporary Application   143

8. **The Spirit's Revolution: Breaking Through the
   Boundaries of Superiority**
   Robert L. Gallagher   **145**
   What's the Purpose?   146
   Panorama Provides the Message   148
   Centurion Conqueror, an Italian Immigrant   149
   Peter's Road Trip in Luke-Acts   151
       Sitting between Bookends of Bigotry   152
       Peter's Broken Road to Jerusalem   154
       Jesus, the Cross-cultural Worker   155
       Jesus's Narrative Twist   155
       Peeling Back Layers of Prejudice   156
       Peter's Rocky Road to Rome   158
   The Spirit's Revolution   159
       The Spirit Presses the Boundaries   160
       The Spirit Pushes the Boundaries   160
       The Early Church and the Law   162
   The Spirit's Boundary Breakers   164
       Cornelius's Vision   165
       Peter's Vision   167
   In the End   169

Conclusion
   Robert L. Gallagher   **171**
   Presentation Summary   172
   Thematic Analysis   174
       Hospitality and Mission   174
       Migration and Mission   175

Contemporary Debates   177
    Interpretative Blind Spot   177
     Women as Faithful Leaders   178
Future Study   180
Jesus the Cross-cultural Worker   181
In Conclusion   182

Author Biographies   **185**

Preface to the American Society of Missiology Series

The purpose of the American Society of Missiology Series is to publish—without regard for disciplinary, national, or denominational boundaries—scholarly works of high quality and wide interest on missiological themes from the entire spectrum of scholarly pursuits relevant to Christian mission, which is always the focus of books in the Series.

By mission is meant the effort to effect passage over the boundary between faith in Jesus Christ and its absence. In this understanding of mission, the basic functions of Christian proclamation, dialogue, witness, service, worship, liberation, and nurture are of special concern. And in that context questions arise, including, how does the transition from one cultural context to another influence the shape and interaction between these dynamic functions, especially in regard to the cultural and religious plurality that comprises the global context of Christian life and mission.

The promotion of scholarly dialogue among missiologists, and among missiologists and scholars in other fields of inquiry, may involve the publication of views that some missiologists cannot accept, and with which members of the Editorial Committee themselves do not agree. Manuscripts published in the Series, accordingly, reflect the opinions of their authors and are not understood to represent the position of the American Society of Missiology or of the Editorial Committee. Selection is guided by such criteria as intrinsic worth, readability, coherence, and accessibility to a range of interested persons and not merely to experts or specialists.

The ASM Series, in collaboration with Orbis Books, seeks to publish scholarly works of high merit and wide interest on numerous aspects of missiology—the scholarly study of mission. Able presentations on new and creative approaches to the practice and understanding of mission will receive close attention.

THE ASM SERIES COMMITTEE

Robert Hunt   Paul Hertig
Robert Gallagher   Kristopher W. Seaman
Hendrik Pieterse   Brian Froehle
Peter Vethanyagamony   Frances Adney
Lisa White

Acknowledgments

We are most thankful for the stellar support and encouragement of Jill Brennan O'Brien, PhD (our editor at Orbis Books), throughout the process of writing our book. Jill's unfailing belief in our project cheered us on toward excellence and completion.

I want to recognize the influence of Richard Slimbach, PhD, a colleague with whom I (Paul) have journeyed in the boundary-breaking enterprise. He relentlessly pushed boundaries while creating and sustaining the Global Studies program at Azusa Pacific University, a program that immerses students in the lives of those culturally different from themselves, producing profound change in their lives.

All research is a community endeavor, and my (Sarita) contributions in *Breaking through the Boundaries* exemplify this truth. As such, I would like to thank Kaleb Pucket, my teaching assistant at George Fox University, for gathering the research materials for this project and editing numerous versions of my manuscript. Additionally, I am grateful to George Fox University for providing a research grant in summer 2014, which made my initial research on Hagar possible.

Introduction

Paul Hertig

We reside in a world of polarities—nation against nation, regime against regime, religion against religion, rich against poor, liberal against conservative, traditional against progressive, residents against nonresidents, inner city against outer city. God's kingdom, however, is not confined by polarities. In God's world we are all in it together. The rain falls on the just and unjust, the sun shines on the righteous and the unrighteous (Mt 5:45). "The God of Jesus is in love with the whole creation."[1] In this human context God's lavish grace becomes a litmus test of the full dimensions of our faith: "The test of faith is whether I can make space for difference. Can I recognize God's image in someone else who is not in my image, whose language, faith, ideas are different from mine? If I cannot, then I have made God in my image instead of allowing him to remake me in his."[2]

In today's context of cultural and religious diversity we still refer to humanity and humankind in the singular.[3] Likewise, interreligious conversation utilizes shared language and imagery, though underlying assumptions may vary greatly. Therefore, we must not assume that we comprehend one representative of a

---

[1] Seán Freyne, *The Jesus Movement and Its Expansion: Meaning and Mission* (Grand Rapids, MI: Eerdmans, 2014), 161.

[2] Jonathan H. Sacks, *The Dignity of Difference: How to Avoid the Clash of Civilizations* (London: Continuum, 2003), 201.

[3] Leo D. Lefebure, *True and Holy: Christian Scripture and Other Religions* (Maryknoll, NY: Orbis Books, 2014), 46.

particular religion, or the religion itself, without deep, ongoing, and meaningful engagement.[4] Every religious tradition has a web of assumptions that are assumed to be normative. When engaged in interreligious conversation, one must also remember that the individual is only one representation of a vast and varied religious faith; thus, there are as many versions of a religion as there are people in that religion.

Consider Christianity, which ranges from Orthodox to Catholicism to Protestantism to nondenominationalism. And, within each of these broad categories runs the gamut from "conservative" to "liberal." Even within Protestantism, one particular denomination, such as the Baptist, ranges from Southern Baptist, to Baptist General Conference, to American Baptist, which differ greatly in theology and practice. Likewise, each religion has a range of viewpoints, theologies, practices, and perspectives.

This is no reason to throw up our hands and say, "What's the point; why even try to understand another religion?" It is best to plunge in, get started, and let authentic engagement begin. When Matthew followed Jesus's call to discipleship, Jesus immediately returned the favor, entered into Matthew's context, and dined with tax-collectors and sinners (Mt 9:9–10). In other words, he immediately entered into the conversation. Jesus did not hesitate to meet people where they were, rather than expecting them to meet him where he was. When Jesus spotted chief tax-collector Zacchaeus up in a tree, he invited him to come down and then stayed at his house that day. Though Zacchaeus was spiritually "lost," this did not prevent Jesus from accepting his hospitality and enter into life-changing conversation (Lk 19:5–10).

Hospitality is often embedded in daily life. "In every culture, hospitality is a sacred duty. It may be an expression of refinement in certain civilisations, but its basic motivation is always religious," observes Pierre-François de Béthune. He adds, "To welcome a stranger is in fact not possible without religious conviction, since it calls for going beyond the immediate reactions common sense dictates. It is natural to be distrustful of a stranger. But every reli-

---

[4] Ibid., 42.

gion has the law of hospitality as a central precept."[5] Hospitality, then, is the place where two religions meet, a place of openness, graciousness, and exchange. If hospitality goes both ways, and here we use the term both literally and figuratively, then such authentic engagement will inform both parties.

The backdrop of many of the texts interpreted in this book center around hospitality: a Midianite priest, Jethro, hears Moses's exodus account, declares that the Lord is greater than all other gods, then offers a sacrifice to God and shares a meal with all the elders of Israel; Gentile Cornelius opens his home to Peter, a Jew, and the Holy Spirit falls on everyone in the home; Boaz and Naomi offer hospitality through a living space, opening up a bright future for Ruth, a migrant widow.

Today our faith, more than ever, "is linked to hospitality: to welcoming the stranger in our midst."[6] De Béthune observes that "hospitality," "hostility," and "hostage" all come from the Indo-European root *host*. This indicates that how we treat the stranger—in our case, the person of a religion different from our own—can potentially go in very different directions.

One can begin the conversation with awareness of God's presence, thus not needing to carelessly rush the conversation in a desired direction, since God is on the scene. A universal longing for the infinite is wrapped up in the religious quest—therefore, common ground among the religions already exists. All religions seek answers to fundamental questions and concerns in the midst of the unknown, the unpredictabilities of life: "Making sense of blessings and misfortunes, good and evil, life and death, and the meaning of life itself is the perennial concern of humanity."[7]

---

[5] Pierre-François de Béthune, *By Faith and Hospitality: The Monastic Tradition as a Model for Interreligious Encounter* (Leominster, UK: Gracewing, 2002), 4, 5.

[6] Ibid., vii.

[7] Anh Q, Tran, "Experience Seeking Faith," in *Christian Mission, Contextual Theology, Prophetic Dialogue: Essays in Honor of Stephen B. Bevans,* ed. Dale T. Irvin and Peter C. Phan (Maryknoll, NY: Orbis Books, 2018), 224.

Therefore, one need not initiate a conversation about the Divine with a Hindu in a way similar to how one might discuss Polynesia with a Mongolian first grader. The first grader may have never heard of Polynesia, and so the discussion begins with a blank slate. But God's revelation was occurring in Hindu society long before Christians arrived on the scene.[8] The whole world is the theater of God's activity (Jn 4:19–24).[9] Thus, the goal is not to win an argument, but to be genuinely present and attentive to the Spirit, laying a foundation for authentic conversation and allowing God to work. Authentic spirituality calls for a loving conversation and a readiness for unpredictable results. Scriptural examples abound of this approach producing surprising results: "Then, leaving her water jar, the woman went back to the town and said to the people, 'Come, see a man who told me everything I ever did. Could this be the Messiah?'" (Jn 4:28–29); "When the young man heard this, he went away sad, because he had great wealth" (Mt 19:22); and "'Lord, I do not deserve to have you come under my roof. But just say the word, and my servant will be healed'" (Lk 7:8).

Therefore, hermeneutics (interpretation and application of scripture) occurs in the zone of the in-between and unexpected. This provides another reason not to throw your arms up in despair. "While misunderstanding seems unavoidable, especially at the beginning, these encounters can be tremendous opportunities for learning if we continue the conversation attentively and learn from our mistakes."[10] Tension is unavoidable, and essential to the process. Each party in a conversation tends to have a mixture of naivete and predispositions; thus, both must be aware of their limitations. Yet, if one approaches the conversation without this humility, and instead responds with defensiveness or insecurity, then the encounter is bound to fail, because it seeks to protect

---

[8] Paul F. Knitter, *Introducing Theologies of Religions* (Maryknoll, NY: Orbis Books, 2002), 72.

[9] David J. Bosch, *Transforming Mission: Paradigm Shifts in Theology of Mission* (Maryknoll, NY: Orbis Books, 1991), 10.

[10] Lefebure, *True and Holy*, 43.

parameters rather than understand the world of the other. A willingness to alter previously held interpretations is essential. When Jesus stepped into Samaria and subsequently into the Samaritan woman's context, the disciples left the scene immediately due to predispositions, and upon returning "were surprised" to find him talking to her (Jn 4:27). One must move past a fear of danger to the potential breakthrough at hand.

For example, when my students in Thailand, observing Buddhists bowing before a representation, asked whether Buddha was being worshiped, one particular monk answered, "No, we are not worshiping Buddha; Buddha said he is not God." Just as Roman Catholics including Mary in prayer and gesture does not indicate they are worshiping her (and they will tell you this), one only finds out these things through inquiry and conversation, not through assumptions.

Historically, biblical interpretation has often defaulted to a "hermeneutics of hostility."[11] Moving from a hermeneutic of hostility to a hermeneutic of hospitality, we come full circle. Plenty of biblical material in both testaments calls for engagement, generosity, and reciprocity with people of cultures and religions different from our own. We now live in a religiously pluralistic world that calls for an updated approach that acknowledges the persistence of multiple religions in our world, and asks how, and in what capacity, we might relate to them. In other words, "to be religious, is to be inter-religious."[12]

A conversation with those of other religious traditions can challenge long-held assumptions, shed new light on biblical perspectives, and open up possibilities for a renewed understanding of the world's religious traditions.[13] Practically speaking, this occurs when we make comparisons and contrasts, helping to provide an understanding of both the religion of the other and of our own. "I do not want to spend my whole life tasting just one fruit. We

[11] Ibid., 49.

[12] Kuncheria Pathil, ed., *Religious Pluralism: An Indian Christian Perspective* (New Delhi: ISPCK, 1991), 348.

[13] Ibid.

human beings can be nourished by the best values of many traditions," writes Thich Nhat Hanh.[14] This respectful exchange can
have a broad impact, and even avert conflict, states Paul F. Knitter:
"There will be no peace among nations unless there is peace and
cooperation among religions."[15]

WHERE DO WE BEGIN?

Charles H. Kraft points out that you cannot study people by
putting them into test tubes. We need to discover people's most
up-to-date beliefs and perceptions of reality by asking ourselves
questions such as, "If I assumed reality to be what they assume it
to be, how would the world look to me? And if it looked that way
to me, how would I behave?"[16] People were born into a particular
society and taught their culture and religion, just as we were born
into our society and taught our culture and religion. "We cannot
legitimately condemn one culture as if it were totally bad or elevate
another culture as if it were totally good."[17] Since religion and
culture are deeply intertwined in most contexts, what does this
say about our way of responding to another religion? Culture and
religion provide coherence and meaning, enabling people to make
sense of their reality. God often shows up in these contexts. This
is evident in three foundational realities: "the revelation of God
in creation, the recognition of the Gentiles' capacity to respond to
the gospel, and the awed awareness that God and his spirit range
far beyond the boundaries of human expectations."[18]

Jesus walked along borderlands and traversed across borders into Gentile regions (Lk 17:11). On his perpetual journey

---

[14] Thich Nhat Hanh, *Living Buddha, Living Christ* (New York:
Riverhead Books, 1995), 2.

[15] Knitter, *Introducing Theologies of Religions*, 245.

[16] Charles H. Kraft, *Anthropology for Christian Witness* (Maryknoll,
NY: Orbis Books, 1996), 12.

[17] Ibid., 76.

[18] Donald Senior and Carroll Stuhlmueller, *The Biblical Foundations
for Mission* (Maryknoll, NY: Orbis Books, 1983), 346.

he engaged in intense theological discussions with a Canaanite woman and a Samaritan woman (Mt 15:21–22; Jn 4:4–7) and, in both cases, encountered them in their brokenness and met their deepest needs. At other times he interacted with the high people of society, such as the centurion in Luke. Prior to healing his servant, Jesus marveled at the centurion's faith, declaring it greater than that in all of Israel (Lk 7:9).

Jesus carried on conversations with skill and sensitivity. Respectful of cultural customs, he followed cultural patterns of protocol and communication. Filling conversations with dialogue, questions, and metaphors, he respected individuals within their cultural contexts in order to associate, reciprocate, and provoke. Since each interreligious context proved to be unique, Jesus contextually tailored his approach to the individual. He often interacted with people even his disciples wanted to avoid. Through humility and vulnerability he created an atmosphere that elicited transparency and transformation.

Jesus responds to the Canaanite woman's expressions of faith and humility with "O woman," which communicates great emotion and respect. Furthermore, Jesus's term for her "great faith" is only used one other time in Matthew, to describe the Gentile centurion.[19] In both of these interfaith encounters Jesus utilizes strong emotion and affirmation to communicate across religious barriers. Jesus literally congratulated the faith of particular individuals who practiced other religions (Mt 8:10; 15:28).

Also surprising is when the Canaanite woman, appealing for healing of her demon-possessed daughter, refers to Jesus as "Lord" three times and even "Son of David" once. The titles Lord and Son of David show respect for the authority of Jesus as healer. After quite a conversation with her, it ends with Jesus literally saying, "Let it be done for you as you wish." He then heals the daughter and acclaims the woman's great faith. This indicates that people of religions other than our own might have deep faith and may be seeking the same God in whom we believe.

---

[19] Warren Carter, *Matthew and the Margins* (Maryknoll, NY: Orbis Books, 2000), 324, 335.

These brief scriptural examples serve only as an introduction to this book, which goes into interpretive detail, chapter by chapter, of specific interreligious encounters, in particular the surprising encounters of religious outsiders and their impact on insiders. Often these amazing interfaith encounters begin with a willingness of both parties to enter the world of the other, even going against the cultural norms of society, reminding us that often we might begin *not* "from a dogmatic starting point but from the human experience of the transcendent other."[20]

We begin the book with an analysis of two stories from Genesis that illustrate our theme of breaking boundaries between God's people and Gentiles. Later chapters conclude with a contemporary application section that ties the insights from the biblical stories to present-day issues of migration and otherness.

CHAPTER SUMMARIES

In Chapter 1 God's universal blessing is expressed *through* Abraham as well as *to* Abraham. While Abraham is himself a stranger in the land, Abraham also extends and receives God's blessing through foreigners. Gentiles such as the Egyptian pharaoh, the Philistine king, Abimelech, and the Canaanite king, Melchizedek, become messengers of truth, correction, and blessing to Abraham. Abraham is both a blessing to the nations and is blessed by the nations.

In Chapter 2 God discloses theological truth directly to and through an Egyptian servant, Hagar. God proclaims a covenantal blessing upon Hagar and her son, and physically saves them from death, providing new insight into the nature and character of God. Evident in God's revelation is unchanging compassion and commitment toward religious outsiders and, by extension, people of all nations. The Hagar account foreshadows God's blessing and revelation to the Gentiles. Through Hagar, a young Gentile

---

[20] Tran, "Experience Seeking Faith," 210.

woman who is socially and religiously marginalized, the people of Israel discover God's faithfulness to humanity.

In Chapter 3, among the dramatic outside-in engagements in the Moses account, Midianite Zipporah circumcises her son while Moses is in Yahweh's death grip, and the spilling of blood identifies Moses as Zipporah's "bridegroom of blood." A Gentile, she not only spares Moses's life, but in the process incorporates her family into the Israelite community. Midianite priest Jethro performs a ritual sacrifice to Yahweh "near the mountain of God" where the ten commandments are given with Moses and family present, while celebrating the exodus and declaring his own faith that "the Lord is greater than all other gods." Furthermore, in the wake of the miraculous exodus from Egypt, Jethro gives practical leadership advice for Moses and the entire Israelite community, "as God so commands" (Ex 18:23).

In Chapter 4 Saul forces David to immigrate to the city of Gath, due to political turmoil within Israel, which provides him an on-going opportunity to intermingle with Gentiles. The case studies of three Philistine movements from Gath show the intersection of migration and mission: Obed-edom, the keeper of the Ark; the Cherethites and Pelethites, King David's Philistine bodyguard; and Ittai, the Gittite warrior-leader loyal to David during Absalom's revolt. All three migrated to Israel and it would appear were brought to some awareness of the Hebrew God. They in turn influenced the evolving destiny of the inhabitants of the city of Jerusalem and the nation of Israel. Thus, mutual migration plays a role in the mission of God—then and now.

In Chapter 5 two widows, Naomi and Ruth, depict a rare and beautiful relationship between a mother-in-law and a migrant daughter-in-law. The two women's stories in the ancient world still illuminate resilient grace and perseverant hope. Facing insurmountable obstacles in patriarchal culture, the two widows cross ethnic boundaries and creatively sustain themselves. The bonding between the two widows transcends the bitterness of loss and turns to triumph when Ruth, a Gentile, finds a patriarchal ally in Boaz, a Jew. Transcending culture and time, the intergenerational and interethnic woman-to-woman relationship restores hope amid insurmountable and darkest moments. Outsiders find their way inside and have a lasting impact.

In Chapter 6 Mordecai and Esther, initially outsiders of Persian King Xerxes's palace, become insiders through spirit-filled, cross-cultural power brokering. They befriend the enemy to carry out their mission of saving their own people. They reverse the power of the "other." King Xerxes changes sides and empowers Esther and Mordecai through twists and turns and multiple reversals in his court. Esther uses the tool of the king's power display, the banquet, to reverse the fate of her people.

In Chapter 7 Magi travel from a unique religious context in Persia, and due to the legends and longings in their own religion, set out on a quest to find and worship "the king of the Jews." In contrast to the religious and political establishments who are disturbed by the news of a cosmic event that announces the birth of the Messiah, the Gentile Magi follow a star and joyfully give gifts to the newborn king. Thus, Jesus is not just "king of the Jews" (Mt 2:2) but king of the entire world.

In Chapter 8 Cornelius's prayers and gifts to the poor ascend as a memorial offering before God (Acts 10:4, 31). Although outside the realm of the church's mission activity this "righteous and God-fearing man" was "respected by all the Jewish people" (Acts 10:22). Therefore, God sends an angel in a vision to honor his Gentile piety. The angel tells Cornelius to send for Peter, who, with a delegation, travels to the home of Cornelius. The Gentile invites them in, and his hospitality results in the Holy Spirit falling upon everyone in the room, both Jews and Gentiles.

It is our hope that the eye-opening scriptures interpreted in each chapter of this book will serve the same transformative purpose today as they did then.

Chapter 1

Abraham:
For the Nations, from the Nations

Sarita Gallagher Edwards

It was a bustling afternoon when I arrived at Union Station in downtown Los Angeles. Departing from my transit train, I weaved through the crowd of commuters as I made my way through the terminal, focused on the day's activities. It was then that an older man approached me in mid-stride and started talking to me. Before I could process what was happening, the man spoke words of God's blessing over me. He proceeded to share a few scriptural passages and then turned away and left. The man's words lingered in the air as he walked away. The whole experience seemed so strange. Who was this man? Why did he come up and bless me in the middle of a train terminal? As I consider the life of Abraham in the book of Genesis, there is a similar feeling of surprise. Who is this Mesopotamian man who just walks into the middle of God's redemptive narrative? Why did God bless him? How did this man from Ur become a blessing to the nations? In this chapter I focus on Abraham's identity as a Mesopotamian migrant as well as his role as a universal representative of God's blessing. This chapter also highlights the person of Abraham, a blessing to and for the nations, who is called to live among the nations and learn from them.

1

ABRAHAM FOR THE NATIONS

The Genesis narrative introduces the reader to Abraham (then called Abram)[1] at the moment of his migrant calling: "Go from your country, your people and your father's household to the land I will show you. I will make you into a great nation, and I will bless you" (Gen 12:1–2). Throughout his lifetime Abraham remains a migrant, traveling as a resident alien rather than settling in one location. The biblical motif of pilgrimage and journey introduced in the Abrahamic narrative foreshadows the future reality of God's people as foreigners in the land (Ex 22:21) and sojourners on earth (2 Cor 5:1–4).

Identity as a Migrant

As Abraham emerges into the biblical narrative, the first promise after his migrant calling is God's declaration to the patriarch that "I [God] will make you into a great nation" (Gen 12:2). This divine promise of nationhood, which includes possession of the land of Canaan and the surrounding region, is repeated to Abraham (Gen 12:7; 15:18–21), his son Isaac (26:2–4), and his grandson Jacob (28:13). God's original blessing upon Abraham in Genesis 12:1–3 additionally includes the promises of divine blessing, fruitfulness, and the affirmation that "all peoples on earth will be blessed through you [Abraham]" (12:3). While Abraham and his household experience these last facets of God's holistic blessing during their lifetimes—material blessing, fruitfulness of the womb and land, and missional blessing—God's covenantal promise of land was not instantly fulfilled in Abraham's life. In Genesis 15, for example, when God reestablishes his covenant

---

[1] The name Abraham is used primarily throughout this chapter instead of Abram for continuity. Additionally, while Sarah is a key participant in the Genesis narrative and in the fulfillment of the Abrahamic blessing (Gen 12:1–3), this chapter focuses primarily on the person and role of Abraham.

with Abraham, the patriarch is able to accept God's promise that he and his wife will conceive a son in their old age—however, the idea that he, Abraham, will possess the land of Canaan continues to stretch Abraham's faith (Gen 15:1–8).

In fact, Abraham does not ever witness the fulfillment of God's promise that his kin will possess the land. Instead, according to the Genesis account, Abraham owns only one piece of land during his life—a field that he purchases from Ephron, son of Zohar the Hittite, which was located in Machpelah near Mamre in Canaan (Gen 23). It is in a cave in the field near Machpelah that Abraham buries his wife Sarah (23:19) and that Abraham himself is later buried by his sons Isaac and Ishmael (26:8–10). While God does later give the Israelite people the land of Canaan (see Josh 1—6), Abraham lives with the tension of a divine promise given, yet not fulfilled. In contrast with his nephew Lot, who settles near Sodom in the plains of the Jordan (Gen 13:10–12), Abraham spends his twilight years constantly moving throughout the land of the Canaanites, Amorites, Hittites, Philistines, and Egyptians.

Abraham's status as a nomadic migrant directly affects his relationship with God. After Abraham is first called by God in Haran, the patriarch enters into a lifelong covenant relationship that requires his full dependency upon God. "Without societal, familial support—even without knowledge of his destination—this nomadic Abram must launch out relying solely and exclusively on Yahweh for direction and sustenance."[2] God's command to Abraham to "go from your country, your people and your father's household to the land I will show you" (Gen 12:1) represents not only a mission of calling, but also an intense learning experience for Abraham among the nations. Gerhard von Rad elaborates that "these three terms indicate that God knows the difficulties of these separations; Abraham is simply to leave everything behind and entrust himself to God's guidance."[3] As a nomadic migrant in

---

[2] Bill T. Arnold, *Genesis* (New York: Cambridge University Press, 2009), 131.

[3] Gerhard von Rad, *Genesis: A Commentary* (Philadelphia: Westminster Press, 1974), 159.

Canaan, Abraham relies upon Yahweh for his physical, economic, relational, and spiritual security. Furthermore, Yahweh uses the nations as tools for discipline and growth in Abraham's life.

Relationships with the Nations

In Abraham's nomadic journey the patriarch interacted frequently with the people living in each area. Abraham made political alliances with (Gen 14:13), fought alongside (Gen 14:1–24), advocated for (Gen 18:16–33), and cut covenants with the local community leaders (Gen 14:13; 21:22–34). While some of Abraham's encounters with foreign leaders created tension, Abraham and his household lived in harmony with the majority of their multicultural neighbors. During his residence in the Promised Land, Abraham lived among almost all the groups of people within the region, including the Canaanites, Perizzites, Egyptians, Hittites, Amorites, and Philistines.

Abraham's presence among the nations enabled him to embody the divine word spoken over his life:

> You will be a blessing.
>   I will bless those who bless you,
>   and whoever curses you I will
>   curse;
>   and all peoples on earth
>   will be blessed through you.
>   (Gen 12:2–3)[4]

God's blessing upon Abraham directly affected his engagements with his foreign neighbors, at times bringing life and at times bringing defeat and death. During Abraham's lifetime God's

---

[4] For additional information regarding the fulfillment of the Abrahamic blessing in the patriarchal lineage, see Sarita D. Gallagher, *Abrahamic Blessing: A Missiological Narrative of Revival in Papua New Guinea* (Eugene, OR: Pickwick, 2014).

blessing is transmitted to Abraham's neighbors primarily through the patriarch's political alliances, as evidenced in Abraham's alliance with the kings of Sodom, Gomorrah, Admah, Zeboyim, and Bela (Zoar) (Gen 14), and in his treaty with King Abimelech of Gerar (21:22–24). Through Abraham, God's curse also came upon the patriarch's neighbors, as experienced by the Egyptian Pharaoh (12:17–20), the kings of Shinar, Ellasar, Elam, and Goyim (Gen 14), and King Abimelech of Gerar (20:1–18). While Abraham may have longed for his own land and independence, Abraham's proximity and interdependence with his foreign neighbors enabled God's prophetic words to be fulfilled during the lifetime of the patriarch.

The Nations as a Blessing to Abraham

While Abraham was the first Gentile called by God and proclaimed a vehicle of God's blessing to the nations (Gen 12:3), Abraham also receives God's correction, blessing, and counsel through his Gentile neighbors. Throughout Abraham's lifetime God uses individuals from outside of the Abrahamic covenant community to serve as God's voice to the patriarch. For example, the Egyptian pharaoh (Gen 12:17–20) and King Abimelech of Gerar (20:1–18) become Abraham's conscience when Abraham lies about his wife, Sarah; Melchizedek, king of Salem, serves as Yahweh's priest, blessing Abraham (14:18–20); and Abimelech, king of Gerar, becomes Abraham's political ally and counsel through a covenantal treaty (21:22–34). Abraham's interactions with the nations are not one-sided. Instead, the foreign kings' and leaders' moral integrity, spiritual alertness, and relationship with Yahweh influence the patriarch's understanding of God.

During Abraham's lifetime God utilizes the nations to teach Abraham about integrity and honor. In Genesis 20:1–18, for example, when Abraham attempts to deceive King Abimelech of Gerar regarding his wife and half-sister, Sarah, it is Abimelech's integrity that attracts the attention of God. In a dream God warns Abimelech not to touch Abraham's wife, Sarah, and the king in his defense declares, "I have done this with a clear conscience and clean hands" (20:5). In response, God agrees with the monarch: "Yes, I know you did this with a clear conscience, and so I have kept you from sinning against me. That is why I did not let you touch her" (20:6). In this episode the lesson of moral integrity and uprightness is taught by the Philistine king, Abimelech, not by the future father of Israel, Abraham. While God fulfills his covenantal promise of protection toward Abraham and his family and curses Abimelech's household, the righteousness of King Abimelech stands in stark contrast with the faithlessness of Abraham. Abraham's belief that there was "no fear of God" (20:11) in Abimelech's household proves to be incorrect. In this narrative it is Abraham, not Abimelech, who fails to fear and honor God. In contrast, it is through the righteous actions of the pagan king, Abimelech, that God is honored and respected.

In the Genesis text Abraham also receives God's blessing from a foreign sovereign, King Melchizedek of Salem. In perhaps one of the most intriguing narratives in scripture, King Melchizedek encounters Abraham after his defeat of King Kedorlaomer and his allies. Melchizedek is identified as the "priest of God Most High" (14:18) and blesses Abraham, prophetically declaring: "Blessed be Abram by God Most High, Creator of heaven and earth. And praise be to God Most High, who delivered your enemies into your hand" (14:19–20). Combining the roles of priest and king, the Canaanite monarch offers a banquet of wine and bread for the returning conqueror, Abraham (14:18).[5] As a priest of God Most High (Hebrew: *El-Elyon*), there is some mystery about Melchizedek's religious background. The divine title God Most High was one of the Hebrew titles used for Yahweh; however, it was also connected to the general Canaanite term for a god, *El*.[6] In the context of the narrative, however, the title God Most

---

[5] Gordon J. Wenham, *Genesis 1—15,* Word Biblical Commentary (Waco, TX: Word Books, 1987), 316.

[6] Claus Westermann, *Genesis 12—36: A Commentary* (Minneapolis, MN: Augsburg Publishing House, 1985), 204.

High most certainly refers to Yahweh. The Canaanite king blesses Abraham with a blessing from God, the "Creator of heaven and earth . . . who delivered your enemies into your hand" (14:19–20). Although Melchizedek is mentioned again in scripture (Ps 110:4; Heb 7), there are no additional details provided about the foreign king's relationship with Yahweh. The reader is simply left with the fact that Abraham is blessed by a Canaanite king who was serving as a priest of Yahweh.

An awareness of the power of God among the nations is evident throughout the Genesis narrative. While Melchizedek is singularly identified as God's priest, the individuals who Abraham encounters are often aware of God's authority and presence. In a later encounter with King Abimelech in Genesis 21, for example, this king of Gerar approaches Abraham to form a political treaty directly because of God's presence with Abraham. In Abimelech's invitation to enter into a treaty, Abimelech explains to the patriarch that "God is with you in everything you do" (21:22). It is for this reason that Abimelech asks to ally himself before God with Abraham: "Now swear to me here before God that you will not deal falsely with me or my children or my descendants. Show to me and the country where you now reside as a foreigner the same kindness I have shown to you" (21:23). In the narrative arc King Abimelech is first introduced as a man of integrity who fears God (Gen 20) and later becomes a man in a covenant relationship with God through Abraham (Gen 21). In the Genesis account King Abimelech's words and actions testify to God's power, sovereignty, and holiness.

Abraham and the Nations: Outside In, Inside Out

By first choosing the Gentile Abraham and then empowering the Gentile leaders in Abraham's life, the universal focus of God's mission becomes evident. God's mission is not restricted to being fulfilled by the covenant people alone. Instead, God's universal blessing is expressed through God's people to the nations, as well as from the nations to God's people. In Genesis, revelation about God is disclosed by foreigners, through Gentiles such as the Egyptian pharaoh; the Philistine king, Abimelech; and the Canaanite king, Melchizedek. Along with Abraham, God adopts these outsiders as messengers of truth, correction, and blessing. While Abraham is himself a stranger in the land, Abraham also extends and receives God's blessing through foreigners.

Abraham's migrant history serves as a foreshadowing of the nation of Israel's future position as foreigners in the land (see Ex 22:21). Just as Abraham was asked to step away from the comforts and support system of his extended family, so "the call of Abram also echoes Israel's later experiences as a people called from Egypt in a great faith experiment in order to travel to an unknown land."[7] The significance of Abraham's nomadic identity, however, extends beyond the future parallel with the exodus narrative. In Abraham's dependence upon God and obedience to God's call, Abraham foreshadows the nature, purpose, and out-working of Israel's ongoing relationship with God. In Abraham's call and life path,

> Israel saw not only an event in her earliest history, but also a basic characteristic of her whole existence before God. Taken from the community of nations (cf. Num. 23:9) and never truly rooted in Canaan, but even there a stranger (cf. Lev. 25:23; Ps. 39:12), Israel saw herself being led on a special road whose plan and goal lay completely in Yahweh's hand.[8]

As such, Abraham is a forerunner of Israel's future position as a stranger in the land, whose well-being and future depend solely on God.

Abraham's nomadic life also reflects the biblical motif of the spiritual pilgrimage. While Abraham did traverse the geographic

---

[7] Arnold, *Genesis*, 131.
[8] Von Rad, *Genesis*, 159.

boundaries of the region, his physical movements mirrored his spiritual relationship with and dependence upon God. Walter Brueggemann explains that Genesis 12:4–9 "introduces the metaphor of journey as a way of characterizing the life of faith. . . . Though the broad outline of geography is to be accepted, the reference to sojourning should not be understood simply as physical movement."[9] Abraham lived a life of faith as he followed God into the land of Canaan and depended upon God for all his needs—physical, economic, political, relational, and spiritual. "The metaphor of journey or sojourn is a radical one. It is a challenge to the dominant ideologies of our time which yearn for settlement, security, and placement."[10] The Abraham narrative thus introduces the concept of human beings' spiritual pilgrimage as they pursue faithful obedience to Yahweh.

The Genesis motif of migration presents an insight into the character and nature of God. Brueggemann notes that the nomadic movement of Abraham's family "is matched by the way of Yahweh himself. Thus Yahweh is understood not as a God who settles and dwells, but as a God who sojourns and moves about (2 Sam 7:4–6)."[11] Just as Abraham traverses borders, so God is not restricted by human-made boundaries. The Genesis narrative emphasizes the universal nature of the *missio Dei* as well as the sovereignty of God over all nations, people groups, and geographic regions. While Abraham's family was previously tied to Mesopotamian deities that were finite and associated with fixed geographic locations, the patriarch and his family are now in a covenant relationship with the almighty, omniscient, living God, who sees, hears, and speaks to all peoples. This leads us to an exploration of the earlier religious background of Abraham as a man from the nations.

---

[9] Walter Brueggemann, *Genesis* (Atlanta: John Knox Press, 1973), 121.

[10] Ibid., 122.

[11] Ibid.

ABRAHAM FROM THE NATIONS

While the Genesis narrative primarily records the life of Abraham after God's call, the motif of God's blessing to the nations is accentuated through Abraham's polytheistic heritage prior to his encounter with Yahweh. In the following section I explore both Abraham's ancestry and his ethnic, national, and religious identities, and how these aspects influence his role among the nations.

Ethnic Identity

In choosing Abraham, son of Terah, God chooses a man from among the nations of ancient Mesopotamia. Abraham's ethnic, national, and religious identities mirror the complexity of the geopolitical climate and the polytheistic religions of the second millennium BCE. While the brevity of the discourse about the sociocultural background of Abraham and his kin in Genesis 11:10–32 may lead the modern reader to assume that the biographical data provided by the author(s) is immaterial to the metanarrative, the opposite is true. Though the theological focus is on "'prophetic history'—history that attempts to read the hand of God into human activities"[12]—the fact that Abraham was a polytheistic foreigner from the heart of Israel's enemies' homeland, ancient Babylon,[13] would have stood out to the original Israelite audience. Just as for twenty-first-century North Americans seeing a person wearing a blue baseball hat embroidered with the white letters "LA" reveals that person's support of Los Angeles Dodgers baseball, so the specific details included in the Genesis 11—12 narrative revealed to the original audience substantial data about Abraham and his family. As such, the patriarch's heritage is not

---

[12] Jonathan Magonet, "Abraham and God," *Judaism* 33, no. 2 (1984): 160–70.

[13] While Abraham lived during the second millennium BCE, the Genesis manuscript was most likely written during the first millennium BCE. The original audience of Genesis, therefore, would have related the city of Ur with ancient first-millennium Babylon.

a sidebar in God's redemptive narrative; instead, it underlines several key theological truths about the nature, purpose, and outworking of God's mission.

The first significant fact that we learn about Abraham, son of Terah, is that he is a direct descendant of Shem, son of Noah (Gen 11:10). This is the same Shem who, along with his brother Japheth, had been told by their brother, Ham, about their father, Noah, lying drunk and unclothed, and respectfully "walked in backward and covered their father's naked body" (9:23). In response to this act of filial piety, Shem and Japheth receive their father's blessing: "Praise be to the Lord, the God of Shem! May Canaan be the slave of Shem. May God extend Japheth's territory; may Japheth live in the tents of Shem, and may Canaan be the slave of Japheth" (9:26–27). In contrast, Ham, father of Canaan, is cursed by his father, Noah, for his disrespectful actions (9:27), a curse that extends to all of Ham's descendants, including Ham's son Canaan.

The Genesis 10:1–32 text goes on to record the lineage of all three of Noah's sons. The descendants of Shem, blessed by Noah, and as such by God, settled in the land from "Mescha toward Sephar, in the eastern hill country" (10:30). The descendants of Canaan, son of Ham, also scattered throughout ancient Mesopotamia, developing into the peoples known as the Amorites, Jebusites, and Hittites, among many other groups. The Canaanite clans later settled in the "land of Canaan," where their territory "reached from Sidon toward Gerar as far as Gaza, and then toward Sodom, Gomorrah, Admah and Zeboyim, as far as Lasha" (Gen 10:18–19). While Noah's descendants, including Abraham, retained their biological connection to their forefather, they developed into new groups with distinct languages, cultural customs, and religious traditions. It is from this multiethnic and multireligious environment that Abraham enters the biblical narrative.

With this historical background the introduction of Abraham, son of Terah, descendant of Shem, begins to make sense theologically. While the inclusion of Abraham in the Genesis 11—12 narrative may at first seem abrupt, God's calling and blessing of Abraham is a continuation of God's active engagement with humanity, specifically with Noah's family. It is in Abraham's encounter with God in Genesis 12:1–3 that God's blessing of Noah and Shem is recalled. In Genesis 12 the narrative of God's blessing is furthered once again, now through Shem's descendant, Abraham. The fulfillment of Noah's curse on the family of Ham (Gen 9:27) is also realized when God promises to give Abraham and his offspring the land of Canaan (Gen 12:6; see also 26:2–4; 28:13). It is from this theological framework of God's blessing and curses that the lineage of Shem is reintroduced in Genesis 11:24–27; this time through Terah, son of Nahor, and his three sons, Abram, Nahor, and Haran.

National Identity

While Abraham is a descendant of Shem, he is simultaneously a foreigner called by God from the heart of ancient Mesopotamia. During the second millennium BCE the city of Ur (modern-day Tell el-Muqayyar in southern Iraq) was a cultural center, both politically and religiously,[14] located on the lower Euphrates River.[15] In the twentieth century archaeological expeditions of Ur, such as that led by British archaeologist Sir C. L. Woolley in 1922, revealed a "great city, cultured, sophisticated, and powerful . . . dominated by a ziggurat, or temple tower" dedicated to the deity Nanna, also known as Sin.[16] The northern Mesopotamian city of Haran was connected to Ur socioculturally, politically, and economically, and was originally "founded as a merchant outpost by Ur"[17] in the third millennium BCE.[18] Located on a small tributary

---

[14] Wenham, *Genesis 1—15*, 272.

[15] Von Rad, *Genesis,* 156–57.

[16] Walter A. Elwell and Philip W. Comfort, eds., *Tyndale Bible Dictionary* (Wheaton, IL: Tyndale House Publishers, 2001), 1281; see also I. Howard Marshall, A. R. Millard, J. I. Packer, and D. J. Wiseman, eds., *New Bible Dictionary*, 3rd ed. (Downers Grove, IL: InterVarsity Press, 1996), 1219.

[17] Tamara M. Green, *The City of the Mood God: Religious Traditions of Harran* (Leiden: Brill, 1992), 19.

[18] Elwell and Comfort, *Tyndale Bible Dictionary*, 571.

of the Euphrates River, the trading city of Haran (which means "crossroads") was situated approximately twenty miles southeast from the ancient city of Edessa (modern-day Urfa, Turkey)[19] in the upper Mesopotamia region known as Aram of the two rivers (Hebrew: *Aram-naharaim*).[20]

In the Hebrew scriptures Abraham and the family of Terah are consistently associated with the Aramean city of Haran (Gen 11:31; 12:4–5; 27:43; 28:10; 29:4). In Deuteronomy 26:5, Abraham and his descendants are further identified as Aramean, a Semitic people who were descendants of Aram, son of Shem (Gen 10:22; see also Deut 26:5). While Abraham later becomes the father of the Israelite people, when God first calls Abraham from Haran, Abraham is an outsider, culturally and religiously, a nomadic foreigner from a polytheistic Aramean community.

Religious Identity

In the Hebrew scriptures there are multiple indications that Abraham and his extended family were influenced by, and on some occasions participated in, the polytheistic religious practices of ancient Mesopotamia. The strongest acknowledgment of the worshiping of gods is evident in the Jewish oral history about the family of Terah: "Joshua said to all the people, 'This is what the Lord, the God of Israel, says: Long ago your ancestors, including Terah the father of Abraham and Nahor, lived beyond the Euphrates River and worshiped other gods'" (Josh 24:2). In the book of Genesis there are also specific details that indicate that the family of Terah participated in idolatry. In Genesis 31:30–35, for example, Rachel, the wife of Abraham's grandson Jacob, is noted as having stolen her father Laban's household idols.

The biographic information provided about the family of Terah in Genesis 11:27–32 also highlights the extent to which

---

[19] D. J. Wiseman, "Haran," in Marshall, Millard, Packer, and Wiseman, *New Bible Dictionary*, 444.

[20] K. A. Kitchen, "Aram, Aramaeans," in Marshall, Millard, Packer, and Wiseman, *New Bible Dictionary*, 66.

Terah's immediate family was embedded in the religious traditions of Mesopotamia. In Genesis 11:27–32 the cities in which Abraham lived, Haran and Ur, and the names of Abram, his wife Sarai, and sister-in-law Milcah, all suggest their association with, and possibly their involvement in, ancient Sumerian religious practices. While contemporary readers may miss the religious connotations embedded in the biographical data, the original Israelite audience, conversant in the multi-religious traditions of their region, would have been cognizant of the references to the Sumerian centers of worship and religious pantheon. As such, the biographical data provided in Genesis 11:27–32 presents more than the biological lineage of Abraham. The details instead introduce the complex religious heritage of Abraham and his family and suggest the extent to which Abraham was exposed to, and potentially was a participant in, the worship of the Sumerian religious pantheon.

First, the two cities in which the family of Terah dwelled, "Ur of the Chaldeans" (Gen 11:28) and Haran (11:31–32), were the two main centers of worship for the Mesopotamian moon god Nanna (also known as Sin). Tamara M. Green explains the significant relationship between these Mesopotamian urban centers and the religious practices associated with lunar god worship:

> In addition to their functions in the spheres of nature and the wider social structure, many deities of the Sumerian and Assyro-Babylonian pantheons exerted political control, even ownership, over particular cities. The god, in turn, intervened with the other divine powers on behalf of his city. . . . Nevertheless, the Moon god's power among his fellow deities and among men extends beyond his local political function at Ur or Harran, for the importance of the moon cult in these states has its origins in the multiple levels of meaning and function of the divine. . . . Sin was not only the Moon god and guarantor of the political order, he was also the guardian deity and ruler of Ur and later the Lord of

Harran, the god to whom these cities appealed and offered their most important prayers.[21]

The Sumerian cult worship of the moon god most likely originally extended from Ur to the outpost of Haran via the trade route that connected Ur in the south with Damascus in the north.[22] From its establishment in the third millennium BCE, the city of Haran gained notoriety as a center of worship for Nanna and his consort, Nikkal.[23] Although Ur and Haran remained the primary religious centers of the Sumerian moon god, the worship of Nanna extended throughout Canaan into Egypt and was only stalled by the Mongol Empire in the thirteenth century CE.[24] Although there is no biblical commentary as to why Terah and his family resided in Ur and Haran, it is an intriguing detail, especially in conjunction with the Sumerian-inspired names of Terah's immediate family members.

The influence of the Sumerian religious pantheon is evident in the given names of Terah's son, Abram, and his daughters-in-law, Sarai and Milcah. Abram's first name, before being renamed Abraham by God, means "[the] father is exalted."[25] As Abraham was first named by his parents, it is probable that his parents were adherents of the moon cult of Ur and Haran; the reference to "father" most likely denotes the father deity Nanna or perhaps another Sumerian deity.[26] The name of Abraham's wife Sarai can also be linked to the Sumerian religious pantheon. Along with her sister-in-law, Milcah, both Sarai and Milcah's names are derivatives of titles given to local female deities. Both forms of the name Sarai and Sarah (Hebrew for "princess"), for example, have their linguistic origin in the Akkadian title of queen *(šarratu)*, which was associated with the goddess Ningal/Nikkal, the consort of

---

[21] Green, *The City of the Moon God*, 35.

[22] Elwell and Comfort, *Tyndale Bible Dictionary*, 571.

[23] Ibid.

[24] Ibid.

[25] Ibid., 6–7.

[26] Ibid.

the moon god Nanna. The name of Sarai's sister-in-law, Milcah (Hebrew for "queen"), is derived from the Akkadian title of princess *(malkātu)*, a title given to the moon god's daughter, the goddess Ishtar.[27] Within the Genesis text the polytheistic heritage of Abram and Sarai's names provide one possible explanation for why God later changed Abram's name to Abraham (Gen 17:5; Hebrew for "father of a multitude"),[28] and Sarai's name to Sarah (Gen 17:14–16; Hebrew for "mother of the nations"). God's renaming of both Abram and Sarai serves as a transition from the couple's polytheistic roots.[29]

In following God's call in Genesis 12:1–3, Abraham transfers his loyalty, culturally and religiously, from the Sumerian religious system to Yahweh. To comprehend the significance of Abraham's decision, it is important to note the holistic provision promised by the Sumerian religious pantheon. Within the Sumerian pantheon of Mesopotamia, the moon god Nanna was identified as an all-knowing, protective deity. The moon god was understood to be a "giver of oracles, [and] guardian of treaties whose eye sees and knows all."[30] The moon god Nanna was said to be the "father of the sun god, Utu (Shamash) and, in some myths, of Inanna (Ishtar), goddess of war and sexual love, and with them formed an astral triad of deities."[31] Associated with the cattle herding of the lower Euphrates River delta, Nanna was represented by a crescent, which was reflective of both the moon and a bull's horns.[32] In addition to these associations, "Nanna bestowed fertility and prosperity on the cowherds, governing the rise of the waters, the growth of reeds, the increase of the herd, and therefore the quantity of dairy products produced. His consort, Ningal [Nikkal]

---

[27] Wenham, *Genesis 1—15*, 273.

[28] Elwell and Comfort, *Tyndale Bible Dictionary*, 6–7.

[29] Ibid.

[30] Green, *The City of the Moon God*, 21.

[31] Kathleen Kuiper, ed., *Mesopotamia: The World's Earliest Civilization* (New York: Britannica Educational Publishing, 2011), 182.

[32] Ibid.

was a reed goddess."[33] While a periphery goddess in the city of Ur, within Haran religious tradition, Ningal/Nikkal is noted as Nanna's spouse.[34]

In choosing to follow God, Abraham transitions from these Sumerian deities, and their promised provision, to Yahweh. While seeds of faith were planted by Abraham's earlier belief in an all-knowing, protective deity (Nanna), Abraham now entrusts his need for protection, fertility of land and womb, and prosperity, to Yahweh. It is noteworthy that God meets Abraham's act of faith by cutting a covenant with the patriarch (Gen 12:1–4; 15) and by promising him land (Gen 12:2, 7; 15:18–21), holistic blessing (Gen 12:2–3; 22:17), fruitfulness of land and womb (Gen 15:4–5; 18:18; 22:17), military dominion and protection (Gen 15:1; 22:17), and missional blessing (12:3; 18:18; 22:18).

Socio-religious Identity

Abraham's polytheistic identity in Genesis identifies Abraham as a man from the nations, culturally and religiously. While Abraham's lineage through Noah's son Shem is one of promised blessing, Abraham was chosen by God from among the peoples of the world as a representative of the nations, for the nations. Yet, in answering God's call, as Bill T. Arnold notes, "Yahweh required Abram to give up the security of his social sanctuary and familial support—so central to ancient tribal sensibilities—in order to depend on Yahweh alone while following this directive."[35]

Abraham's calling turns the audience's attention toward God, who alone is holy, as Abraham's faith reaches its climax. It is God who initiates a covenant relationship with the patriarch, not Abraham. The lack of narration regarding God's rationale for choosing Abraham shifts the narrative emphasis away from

---

[33] Ibid.

[34] Green, *The City of the Moon God*, 27.

[35] Arnold, *Genesis*, 131.

the unknown character of Abraham to the universal purposes of God. As von Rad explains:

> And now follows the new point of departure in the divine revelation of salvation: an address to a man amidst the multitude of existing nations, a constraining of this one man for God and his plan of history by virtue of a free act of choice. Why God's choice did not fall upon Ham or Japheth, but rather upon Shem, and within Shem upon Arpachshad, and within the descendants of Arpachshad upon Abraham, the narrator does not explain. Yahweh is the subject of the first verb at the beginning of the first statement and thus the subject of the entire subsequent sacred history.[36]

There is no confusion in the Genesis text; the sole author, instigator, and maintainer of Israel's redemptive history is God. While Abraham plays a large role in the outworking of God's salvific plan, his role reflects his obedience and submission to God and God's universal mission (Gen 12:3).

CONCLUSION

In the book of Genesis, Abraham's presence among the nations facilitates the fulfillment of God's words spoken over Abraham's life: "You will be a blessing. I will bless those who bless you, and whoever curses you I will curse; and all peoples on earth will be blessed through you" (Gen 12:2–3).[37] In encountering the person of Abraham the reader meets a foreigner; a Mesopotamian man from a polytheistic community whose very name recalls the Sumerian religious pantheon. While Abraham's lineage can be traced to Shem, the patriarch's ethnic, national, and religious identities reflect his Mesopotamian heritage. Abraham's background,

---

[36] Von Rad, *Genesis,* 159.

[37] For additional information regarding the fulfillment of the Abrahamic blessing in the patriarchal lineage, see Gallagher, *Abrahamic Blessing.*

however, is not a drawback to God's redemptive mission. God's desire to reach out to all humanity is reflected in God's selection of Abraham. Abraham's status as a nomadic migrant also enables the patriarch's ongoing interaction with his foreign neighbors, through whom he receives God's correction, blessing, and counsel, furthering the fulfillment of the Abrahamic blessing of Genesis 12:1–3. Abraham becomes a living representation of God's love for the nations. In choosing Abraham, God chooses a man from the nations to be God's blessing to the nations.

Chapter 2

Missional Revelation through the Story of Hagar the Egyptian

Sarita Gallagher Edwards

It was a humid evening in Port Moresby, the capital city of Papua New Guinea. My Bible School colleagues and I had just finished playing a pickup game of soccer with an energetic group of young girls from the neighborhood. While the improvised soccer field was not quite a rectangle and the sun always seemed to set before the game ended, our Friday afternoon games were always filled with excitement and laughter. Now, leaning back on a makeshift wooden deck as the last rays of light faded, the girls animatedly told stories about their day. During the past few weeks I'd gotten to know and appreciate each of these girls. One young girl in particular quickly became my companion. At fourteen years old, Mary was of slight stature, her long dark hair indicating her Central Province heritage.[1] Initially quiet and reserved, Mary soon became an enthusiastic conversationalist and radiated a kindness and gentleness that earned her the respect of her peers. Over the weeks that followed, Mary and a few of her close friends and I would often tell stories long into the afternoon under the shade of a mango tree.

---

[1] The name Mary is a pseudonym.

As my time in Papua New Guinea drew to a close, my attendance at the weekly soccer games became more sporadic. It was thus with great joy that a week before my departure, I opened my apartment door to see several of the girls. Hearing that I was leaving the city, they had come to say goodbye. We chatted for a few minutes before I realized that Mary was not a part of the group. When I asked where Mary was, the answer stopped me in my tracks. As the whole story came out, my heart sank and I began to feel physically ill. Mary had gotten married. At fourteen years of age, Mary's parents had accepted an offer of marriage given by an Australian expatriate in his sixties living in Papua New Guinea. According to the cultural customs of Central Province, the groom paid a large bride price to the bride's family. Bride prices in this region traditionally exceed US$20,000 in money and goods, and as such could provide temporary financial security for the entire extended family. Nevertheless, a marriage with such a large age difference was highly unusual in the region. Filled with sadness, I desperately wanted to rectify the situation for this young girl. What kind of person would take advantage of an impoverished family desperate to survive? What kind of man would marry a girl who was barely a teenager?

In the Hebrew scriptures there is a similar story of injustice and exploitation of a young woman in Genesis. As a domestic slave in the household of Abraham and Sarah, Hagar left her Egyptian homeland as a young girl, joining her nomadic Hebrew masters. It is from this position of powerlessness that Hagar was given to her master, Abraham, in order to bear Sarah, her barren mistress, a son. The story of Hagar is primarily interpreted as it relates to the lives of her Hebrew masters, Abraham and Sarah. As such, the biblical narrative of Hagar is often reduced to a strategic mistake in the lives of Abraham and Sarah, with Hagar's son Ishmael becoming a false answer to God's covenant promise to Abraham. The biblical narrative, however, reveals a more complex story of God's faithfulness, one of God's faithfulness to Abraham and Sarah but also to Hagar and Ishmael.

In the Genesis narrative God is presented as the God of all nations, not limited by geographical boundaries and not biased toward a certain ethnicity, gender, age, or social status. In God's interactions with Hagar, an enslaved foreigner from a polytheistic background, God reveals a steadfast commitment to bless all the peoples of the world. The story of Hagar serves as a compact example of God's universal mission to the nations. In this chapter I explore Hagar's position as one blessed by God as well her role as an agent of God's revelation to the Hebrew people. In addition, I will highlight the missional motifs within the Hagar narrative that emphasize God's sovereignty over all peoples, God's faithfulness to humanity, and the universal nature of God's mission.

HISTORICAL BACKGROUND

When considering Hagar's journey, there are several sociocultural and ethical questions that arise. For example, was it culturally appropriate in the ancient Near East[2] to ask a servant woman to sleep with one's husband? What was the appropriate relationship between a female servant and her mistress? And what were the hereditary rights of a concubine and her offspring? From a twenty-first-century Western perspective, customs such as concubinage, polygamy, polytheism, and slavery are difficult to understand. Although one could dismiss these elements as superfluous to the narrative, it is in comprehending these sociocultural factors that God's actions are put into perspective. Of particular significance in Hagar's story are the practices of concubinage, slavery, and polytheism.

The adoption of Hagar as a concubine comes during a time of desperation on the part of Sarah and Abraham. Almost eleven

---

[2] The ancient Near East during the time of the patriarchs encompassed the ancient civilizations of Mesopotamia (modern Iraq and Syria), Persia (modern Iran), Anatolia/Asia Minor (modern Turkey), Egypt, and the Levant (modern Israel, Palestine, Jordan, Syria, and Lebanon).

years after following God into the land of Canaan, Sarah and
Abraham still await their long-promised son. In the ancient Near
East, as in many parts of the world today, children were seen as
gifts from God, bringing honor, financial security, and longevity
to their parents' name. Furthermore, "for a married woman to
be without children in the patriarchal world is a misfortune of
overwhelming proportions. Only the birth of a child can bring
relief."[3] As such, Sarah, now in her mid-seventies, encourages
her husband, Abraham, himself in his mid-eighties, to alleviate
this social and personal pain.[4] Sarah directs Abraham to take
her personal slave Hagar as a concubine to continue Abraham's
family lineage.

The practice of taking a concubine to produce male heirs was
a "common and accepted one in the ancient Near East."[5] Sarah's
suggestion is therefore not unusual in this context. The tradition of concubinage was widely practiced throughout the Fertile
Crescent region. In Mesopotamia, Abraham's own place of birth,
it was permitted for a man to "have legal sexual relations with
slaves. In [nearby] Assyria the husband was able to take several
free-born concubines . . . although the 'concubine' was subject to
the wife's authority."[6] According to the ancient Babylonian laws of
Hammurabi, again from the region of Abraham's birth, the sons
of a concubine were able to share in their father's inheritance,
and concubines, even if inclined to arrogant behavior, could be
treated as slaves but not sold.[7] It was thus no surprise that Sarah,
according to Mesopotamian custom, introduces Hagar to Abraham as the culturally appropriate solution to their childlessness.

---

[3] Claus Westermann, *Genesis 12—36: A Commentary* (Minneapolis,
MN: Augsburg, 1985), 237.

[4] Ibid.

[5] John Barton and John Muddiman, *The Oxford Bible Commentary*
(Oxford: Oxford University Press, 2001), 51.

[6] J. A. Thompson, "Concubine," in *The New Bible Dictionary*, ed.
I. Howard Marshall, A. R. Millard, J. I. Packer, and D. J. Wiseman (Grand
Rapids, MI: Eerdmans, 1996), 219.

[7] Ibid.

As contemporary readers of the Genesis text, we often feel a sense of familiarity with the person of Hagar. Hagar's position as a slave, however, is actually quite foreign to modern readers. Most likely born or sold into slavery as a young child, Hagar was presumably purchased by Abraham or given to him as a gift during his residence in Egypt (see Gen 12:10–20). Ten years later, when Hagar is presented to Abraham as a viable second wife, Hagar would have still been relatively young. Hagar's youth is evident in that she is still unmarried and within her childbearing years. As represented in the narrative, Hagar is the legal property of Sarah, who was free to present Hagar to her husband as his concubine.[8] The fact that Sarah chooses Hagar to carry Abraham's child suggests a possible level of relationship and trust between the two women.[9] This positive assumption, however, may simply be a twenty-first-century projection, as according to ancient Near Eastern customs, Hagar had no option but to obey the orders of her mistress. As a slave, Hagar was legally bound to serve her masters obediently and succumb to any demand. Hagar's status as a bondservant placed her in the lowest tier of the social hierarchy, with limited rights and a limited destiny. In all eyes except God's, Hagar was a person of little consequence.

What Hagar remembered of her Egyptian homeland is unknown. The narrator's repeated reference to "Hagar the Egyptian" (Gen 21:9) suggests that Hagar retained portions of her Egyptian tradition—possibly her native language and various religious and social customs. The notation that each time Hagar fled Abraham's encampment she headed straight toward Egypt supports the hypothesis that Hagar retained a sense of Egyptian identity. Whether or not Hagar remained culturally and religiously Egyptian, her encounter with Yahweh suggests that she had limited or possibly no exposure to the Hebrew God.[10] When Hagar encounters

---

[8] Robert Alter, *Genesis: Translation and Commentary* (New York: Norton, 1996), 67.

[9] Westermann, *Genesis 12—36*, 238.

[10] While the original author(s) indicate in the Genesis 16 text that Hagar encountered Israel's God (Hebrew: *Yahweh*), it is unclear whether

Yahweh in the wilderness of Shur, it is significant that she does not identify the messenger of the Lord with any of deities within the Egyptian pantheon (Gen 16:13). How did Hagar know that the angel speaking to her was not a representative of the Egyptian god Ra (the sun god), Isis (the goddess of life), or Osiris (the god of the dead)? Perhaps adhering to the ancient worldview that deities were geographically restricted, Hagar considered it impossible for the gods of Egypt to retain their power outside of Egypt's borders. It was in this polytheistic context that Hagar identifies Yahweh as a new god—"I have now seen the One who sees me" (Gen 16:13)—a god who sees her plight; a god whose power and authority extend beyond regional borders, even in the wildernesses of Shur and Beersheba; a god not restricted to a temple, not facilitated by priests, nor solely represented by a king. By understanding Hagar's desperate plight and her religious worldview, Hagar's relief in encountering such a god is understandable, a God who is personal rather than distant, all-powerful rather than geographically restricted, and aware of all humanity rather than only the socially elite.

HAGAR AS A THEOLOGIAN

The narrative of Hagar reveals the mission of God on multiple levels. First, in the Genesis 16 narrative it is Hagar, a foreign-born Egyptian slave, not Abraham or Sarah, who declares a theological truth about the character and person of Yahweh. In the Hebrew scriptures Hagar is the second person, after Melchizedek (Gen

---

or not Hagar had previous knowledge of the God of Abraham and Sarah. In the narrative Hagar uses the generic term for "god" (Hebrew: *El*) to describe the deity she encounters: "She gave this name to the Lord [Yahweh] who spoke to her: 'You are the God [El] who sees me'" (16:13). Although the narrative is not explicit, Hagar's act of naming God, in addition to the wider context of the narrative, suggests that Hagar was most likely engaging with Yahweh for the first time on the road to Shur (Gen 16:7–14).

14:18), to ascribe a name to God.[11] Hagar and Melchizedek are both outside of the lineage of Abraham, the forerunner of the Israelites. For the original Hebrew audience the naming of God by a female foreigner would have directly challenged the preconceptions and prejudices that many Hebrews held toward both women and non-Israelites. The inclusion by the author(s) of this narrative, therefore, does not reflect the common worldview of the Israelites; instead, it depicts the independent actions of God. It is God, not Abraham or the Israelite audience, whose compassion and mission extend beyond Israel.

Hagar the Egyptian identifies the true nature of Yahweh by naming God *El Roi,* "the God who sees me" (Gen 16:13). While spoken by a foreign-born concubine, this theological truth is remembered by the Israelites for posterity in the biblical text and also in the naming of Hagar's well, *Beer Lahai Roi,* which means "Well of the Living One who sees me" (v. 14). While Hagar names God "the God who sees me" (v. 13), the seeing is mutual, as Hagar also "sees" God. In the narrative God sees Hagar's plight and allows Hagar to "see" and "hear" him through the angel, which reveals again God's all-encompassing compassion toward this desperate woman. The geographic location of Hagar's first encounter with God, the Desert of Shur, adds to the motif of "seeing" as Shur, which means "wall" in Hebrew, and "could also be construed as a verb that occurs in poetic texts, 'to see' . . . and may relate to the thematics of seeing in Hagar's story."[12]

While Hagar is the first woman to make a theological declaration about God, she is followed by a list of women who proclaim theological truth about God and/or serve as prophetesses of Yahweh, including Miriam (Ex 15:1–21), Deborah (Judg 4—5), Hannah (1 Sam 2:1–10), Huldah (2 Kgs 22:14), Elisabeth (Lk 1:41–45), Mary (Lk 1:46–55), and Anna (Lk 2:36–28). In the Hebrew canon women often serve as a vehicle for the voice of

---

[11] Additional individuals who ascribe a name to God and/or name a place of worship include Jacob (Gen 33:20), Moses (Ex 17:15), Gideon (Judg 6:23–24), and Ezekiel (Ezek 48:35).

[12] Alter, *Genesis,* 69.

God, proclaiming God's truth to the male leaders of the day. Although Hagar has the additional cultural barriers of a low socioeconomic class and foreign birth, it is her gender that perhaps divides her the most from the patriarchy of her time. In Hagar's two encounters with God in the wildernesses of Shur and Beersheba (see Gen 16:1–16; 21:14–21), the reader is made aware that God sees, listens to, and acts on behalf of a woman, one who is also a slave and foreigner.

God's choice of self-revelation to Hagar, an Egyptian female servant, exemplifies God's ongoing commitment to extend lovingkindness to all peoples. In the Old Testament, Hagar's encounters with the angel of God in the wildernesses of Shur and Beersheba are reminiscent of the prophet Elijah's encounters with the Sidonian widow in Zarephath (1 Kgs 17:8–16, 17–24). In each narrative God's messengers are led by God to foreign women who are in distress. While the specific contexts of the stories are unique, God blesses each woman and her son and provides them with guidance and the sustenance to survive.[13] In both meetings the women respond to God with great acts of faith and obedience, Hagar returning to her mistress Sarah (Gen 16:9–15), and the Sidonian widow, in a position of imminent starvation, giving a portion of her family's last meal to the prophet Elijah (1 Kgs 17:13–16). Later, when the women's sons once again face death, God brings both boys back from the brink of death, and, in the case of the Sidonian widow's son, back from death.[14]

In the Gospel of Luke, Jesus emphasizes the theological significance of God's intervention in the life of the Sidonian widow. Addressing the Nazareth synagogue, Jesus states: "I assure you that there were many widows in Israel in Elijah's time, when the sky was shut for three and a half years and there was a severe famine throughout the land. Yet Elijah was not sent to any of

---

[13] In the Sidonian widow narrative, the miracle of the jar of oil that never ran dry was also a representation of God's blessing, as oil was considered by the Hebrews to be a symbol of God's blessing (see Jer 31:12; Heb 1:9).

[14] For Hagar and Ishmael, see Genesis 21:14–21; for the Sidonian widow and her son, see 1 Kings 17:17–24.

them, but to a widow in Zarephath in the region of Sidon" (Lk 4:24–26). As Jesus notes to the first-century Galilean audience, the Sidonian widow narrative exemplifies that God's lovingkindness and compassion extend beyond the borders of Israel. Yahweh, the God of Israel, sees, hears, and acts with compassion toward the "other."

In the New Testament the depiction of the woman at the well (Jn 4:1–42) also contains parallels with the Hagar narrative. As shown in Table 2-1, whether it is an intentional comparison made by the Johannine author or not, both women share parallel relational and social statuses, foreign heritage, and unique encounters with the Godhead. While the two women are on the social margins of their communities, they have a theological revelation about God that contributes to humanity's understanding of the Divine.

The motif of women at wells extends beyond the Hagar[15] and Samaritan narratives to include the matriarchs Rebekah (Gen 24:11–16), Rachel (Gen 29:2–10), and Zipporah (Ex 2:16–22). In the biblical metanarrative these encounters hold spiritual significance because "a well is a primary source of water in a dry region and is thus readily identifiable as a source of blessing (cf. Jn 4:7–10)." In addition to water being a symbol of life, prosperity, and God's blessing, "the fact that a well is open to all and that anyone may drink from it suggests the universal nature of the blessings spoken there."[16] In the narratives of Hagar and the Samaritan woman that is indeed the case; both women witness the universal intent of God's mission in their encounters. As depicted in Table 2-1, Hagar and Ishmael receive the fulfillment of God's blessing upon humankind, and the woman at the well, a person of Samaritan heritage, encounters the promised Messiah, "the Savior of the world" (Jn 4:39).

---

[15] In the Hagar narrative the angel of God first encounters Hagar by the spring along the road to Shur (Gen 16:7) and later opens Hagar's eyes to see a well of water in the Desert of Beersheba (Gen 21:19).

[16] John H. Sailhamer, vol. 1, *Genesis-Leviticus,* in *The Expositor's Bible Commentary,* rev. ed., gen. ed. Tremper Longman III and David E. Garland (Grand Rapids, MI: Zondervan, 2008), 177.

Table 2-1. Parallels between Hagar and the Woman at the Well

Parallel Motifs	Hagar (Genesis 16, 21)	Woman at the Well (John 4:1–42)
Heritage	Egyptian	Samaritan
Rejected by her husband(s)	16:6; 21:14	4:17–18
Social outcast	21:14	4:4–7 (implied)
Encountered God	Angel of the Lord/God	Jesus Christ
Given a theological insight about God	"the God who sees me" (16:13)	"Then Jesus declared, 'I, the one speaking to you—I am he [the Messiah]'" (v. 26). "He told me everything I ever did" (v. 39).
Universal blessing of God revealed	"The angel added, 'I will increase your descendants so much that they will be too numerous to count'" (16:10).	"They said to the woman, 'We no longer believe just because of what you said; now we have heard for ourselves, and we know that this man really is the Savior of the world'" (v. 42).

MISSIONAL MOTIFS IN THE HAGAR NARRATIVE

In the Hagar narrative God's universal mission to the nations is also evident in the missional themes of the text. In the following section I highlight the motifs of (1) God's sovereignty over all peoples, (2) God's faithfulness to humanity, and (3) the universal nature of God's mission.

God's Sovereignty over All Peoples

It is through Hagar's encounter with Yahweh that God's authority over all peoples is revealed. While the episode is a microcosm of God's missional intent, the wider context of the Genesis narrative reveals a God who is sovereign over all lands and peoples. The Hagar narratives of Genesis 16 and 21 are a part of the broader literary motif of God's involvement with foreign leaders and nations. During Abraham's migration through the land of Canaan, Egypt, and Philistia, God interacted on four separate occasions with foreign kings, cities, and individuals (from the most powerful ruler of the region, the Egyptian pharaoh, to one of the least significant individuals in society, Hagar). God's engagement with foreigners encompassed the rich and poor, nations and cities, kings and slaves, and men and women. Listed in the Genesis text from the most powerful to least powerful, the four encounters in Genesis 12—21 include God's interaction with the Egyptian pharaoh (Gen 12:10–20), Sodom and Gomorrah (Gen 19), the Philistine King Abimelech of Gerar (Gen 20), and the Egyptian servant, Hagar (Gen 16 and 21).

In each of the cross-cultural encounters, God engages with the foreigners. In the first two narratives God's intervention led to judgment and destruction of the king of Egypt and the Dead Sea region, respectively. In the narrative of Abraham's deception of the Egyptian pharaoh the narrator recorded that "the Lord inflicted serious diseases on Pharaoh and his household because of Abraham's wife Sarai" (Gen 12:17). Pharaoh's household was so negatively affected by pharaoh's obtainment of Abraham's wife that the pharaoh, upon finding out about Abraham's deception, immediately expelled Abraham from the region (Gen 12:18–20). Later, when the moral depravity of Sodom and Gomorrah reached God, God destroyed the two cities. In speaking with Abraham before the impending destruction, God explained, "The outcry against Sodom and Gomorrah is so great and their sin so grievous that I will go down and see if what they have done is as bad as the outcry that has reached me" (Gen 18:20–21). In both the narratives of the Egyptian pharaoh and that of "the cities of the plain," God brought punishment upon a spectrum of arenas: an Egyptian monarch and his nation, and two Moabite cities. In these encounters the dominion of God over all nations, geographic regions, and peoples is emphasized. The God of Abraham is identified through these episodes as the judge and sovereign of the world, not just of the Hebrew people.

While God's engagement with foreigners in Genesis sometimes brought judgment, God's encounters also brought redemption. The two episodes in the Genesis 12—21 sequence that illustrate God's lovingkindness to outsiders include God's supernatural intervention in the lives of King Abimelech of Gerar (Gen 20) and Hagar the Egyptian (Gen 16; 21). In Genesis 20 Abraham repeats his marital deception involving his wife and half-sister Sarah and consequently brings God's judgment upon his ally King Abimelech of Gerar. In the case of Abimelech, however, God personally warns the local sovereign of the impending divine judgment through a dream (Gen 20:3–7). Within this dream God acknowledges Abimelech's innocence and explicitly points out the divine protection of Abimelech. God speaks to Abimelech and explains, "Yes, I know you did this with a clear conscience, and so I have kept you from sinning against me. That is why I did not let you touch her" (Gen 20:6).

Again, in the narrative of Hagar the Egyptian, God intervenes with words of prophetic blessing and the provision of water and survival. In these two narratives, God is revealed to be a God of both justice and mercy. God acknowledges the innocence of Abimelech and the powerlessness of Hagar and intervenes supernaturally on their behalf, ensuring their salvation. Even in the midst of God's covenantal relationship with Abraham and his kin,[17] God continues to be the God of all nations. While God honors the original covenantal promise to Abraham that he would "bless those who bless you, and whoever curses you I will curse" (Gen 12:3), God's judgment and compassion are simultaneously local and universal in focus.

The structural placement of the Hagar narrative purposefully creates a thematic climax within God's engagements with foreigners in Genesis 12—21. While the story of Hagar could be cast aside as an example "of the threat to the fulfillment of the promise that Abraham will have a legitimate heir by his wife Sarah" and the subsequent "setting aside of that threat (cf. 15:2–4),"[18] this explanation overlooks the structural buildup toward the Hagar narrative. In addition to exemplifying God's sovereignty over king and slave, city and nation, men and women, the four cross-cultural narratives document an increasingly intimate relationship between God and the individuals involved. The author(s) record the movement of God from the distant judgment of the Egyptian pharaoh (Gen 12:10–20) to God's involved conversation preceding the judgment of the cities of Sodom and Gomorrah (Gen 18); and then from God's protection of Abimelech through a dream (Gen 20) to God's prophetic blessing and care of Hagar and her son through an angelic encounter (Gen 16; 21). As these examples move from the most powerful to the most powerless, God's involvement and protection increase. While it can be tempting to conclude that God simply loves the outcast more than the mighty, this is an oversimplification of the narratives. In this sequence the author(s) are addressing a broader theme that extends throughout the Genesis text—that God actively engages with all nations and

---

[17] While God's covenant with Abraham is first initiated by God in Genesis 12:1–4, the covenant promise is repeated throughout the Genesis text (see 12:7; 18:17–18; 22:15–18; 26:2–5).

[18] Barton and Muddiman, *The Oxford Bible Commentary*, 51.

that God's omnipotence, justice, and mercy extend toward all the communities of the world.

God's Faithfulness to Humanity

In the Hagar narrative we witness one of the most intimate examples in the Old Testament of God's concern for a person outside of the Abrahamic covenant. God is presented as a God who speaks, listens to, and sees human beings in the midst of their suffering and hardships. While God is demonstrated to be all-seeing and all-merciful, the individuals whom God interacts with are depicted as fallible, self-seeking, and judgmental. In the midst of the ensuing domestic drama, one specific missional theme surfaces: God's faithfulness in the face of humanity's unfaithfulness. While as a reader it is tempting to take sides in the marital dispute between the barren Sarah and her servant Hagar, the original narrator made no such claims. In the narratives of Genesis 16 and 21 there are no clear distinctions between hero and villain. Similar to the twists and turns of a modern-day television soap opera, the familial details of Abraham and Sarah's interactions with the maidservant Hagar are multilayered and complex. While Hagar is legally in a position of servitude, the original author(s) have no qualms in mentioning Hagar's inappropriate treatment of her childless mistress (Gen 16:4). Likewise, while apparently holding a good opinion of Hagar prior to her betrothal to Abraham, Sarah similarly despises Hagar once pregnant (Gen 16:5–6). Abraham, caught in the middle of this domestic quarrel, is also blameworthy; he sets the entire episode into motion when he follows his wife's misguided advice (Gen 16:3–4). By taking Hagar as his wife, Abraham deviates slightly from his greatest fear that a servant from his household will be his heir (Gen 15:1–3). Now, through the intervention of his wife, Sarah, Abraham's heir will be born of a servant from his household. In the sequence of events it becomes clear that the author(s) of the narrative did not support the actions of Abraham, Sarah, or Hagar.

To emphasize the moral fallibility of Abraham, Sarah, and Hagar, the author(s) allude to the Genesis creation narrative to solidify their point. "These allusions are clearly intentional and help shape the narrative and provide its primary connection to the larger themes of the book: faith and obedience."[19] In both narratives the protagonists, Adam and Eve (Gen 3), and Abraham and Sarah (Gen 16), attempt to invoke blessing upon themselves independent of God. In Genesis 3:6, for example, Adam and Eve endeavor to find wisdom apart from God, and in Genesis 16:1–4 Abraham and Sarah try to bring about the promised son. John H. Sailhamer explains:

> Eve desired the fruit she believed would make her wise, so she took the fruit, gave it to her husband, and he ate. Similarly, Sarai desires a son from whom she hopes "her house will be built." So she takes Hagar and gives her to her husband, Abraham. Sarai's words ("perhaps I [my house?] will be built from him") point to the promised "seed" of Abraham in the earlier narratives. God had not given him a son, and the only one to possess his inheritance will be "a son of [his] house."[20]

As illustrated in Table 2-2, the parallel between the two narratives continues as God questions Hagar, as he did previously with Adam and Eve. God also blesses each party, and names humankind and later Ishmael and Isaac. In each episode God responds to the dubious actions of each person with kindness and compassion. While the natural consequences of each party's actions still unfold, God's blessing remains steadfast. In each account God's blessing continues to the next generation despite the impudent actions of its present recipients.

God's faithfulness is further highlighted in the parallel structure of the Genesis 16 and 21 narratives (see Table 2-3). In each episode, both stories are organized into two parts: Abraham and Sarah's response to their childlessness, and God's response to their

---

[19] Sailhamer, *Genesis-Leviticus,* 175.
[20] Ibid.

Table 2–2. Parallels between the Creation and Hagar Narratives

Parallel Motifs	Creation Narrative	Hagar Narrative
Action apart from God	Adam and Eve attempt to find wisdom apart from God (Gen 3:6).	Abraham and Sarah attempt to produce the "promised son" apart from God (Gen 16:1–4).
God's questioning	God questions Adam and Eve (3:9–13).	Angel of God questions Hagar (16:8; 21:17, 18).
God's blessing	God blesses humankind [male and female] (1:28; 5:2).	God blesses Abraham and Hagar's son (16:10–12; 21:13) and Abraham and Sarah's son (26:2–5).
God's naming	God names them "humankind" (5:2, NET).	God names Hagar's son Ishmael (16:11) and Sarah's son Isaac (17:19).

actions. The patriarchal and divine responses are divided into three subsections, in which both groups speak, listen, and see. The matriarch, Sarah, who is a primary instigator in both periods of domestic conflict,[21] is cast in a very negative light as she takes matters into her own hands and tries to generate the promised child through her servant's womb. However, Sarah is not alone in her miscalculation of the situation. Abraham is a willing accomplice

---

[21] It was Sarah who first told Abraham to take Hagar as his wife (16:2) and who later requested that Hagar and Ishmael be cast out of the Hebrew encampment (21:10).

in the scheme as he heeds Sarah's advice, agrees to take Hagar as his wife, and then later fails to protect the now pregnant Hagar from being mistreated in his household (Gen 16:2–6). Hagar also is not blameless in this familial drama. As mentioned previously, Hagar is accused of viewing her mistress with disdain once pregnant, and even her son, Ishmael, joins the action when he mocks his half-brother, Isaac (Gen 16:5; 21:9). As the drama unfolds, it becomes clear that Sarah speaks; Abraham listens; and Hagar, Ishmael, and Sarah see without wisdom. The result is an all-encompassing view of the fallenness and fallibility of each participant. Not one individual emerges above the petty drama. All are portrayed as flawed and motivated by self-seeking desires.

God's response in Genesis 16 and 21 stands in contrast with the unsympathetic portrayal of the human participants. God engages with the patriarch and his wives with lovingkindness, continuing the threefold pattern of speaking, listening, and see-ing. The author(s) purposefully contrast the lack of forgiveness and disdain of Sarah and Hagar with the kindness of God, who speaks words of blessing, listens with compassion, and sees the suffering of each human being. The disparity between depictions could not be more profound. At the height of Hagar's shame and rejection, Yahweh speaks to, listens to, and sees Hagar. Similarly, God does not punish Sarah or Abraham for their ill-fated plan to produce a child.

This juxtaposition between the faithfulness of God and the faithlessness of human beings emphasizes that it is God who is the true hero of the narrative. As evidenced in the parallel structures of the Genesis 16:1–16 and 21:1–21 passages, the principal intent of the author(s) in recounting this familial conflict is theological. While God calls Abraham from Haran and cuts a covenant to bless Abraham and his household for posterity, God's love is universal in its breadth, extending to the rich and poor, male and female, slave and free, to those outside the Abrahamic covenant as well as to those within. It is God, not humankind, who is consistently blameless, faithful, loving, and forgiving.

Table 2-3. Parallels between the Hagar Narratives

Human Response

Genesis 16:1–16		Genesis 21:1–21
SPEAKS	**Sarah speaks**	**Sarah speaks**
	"Go sleep with my slave; perhaps I can build a family through her" (v. 2).	"Get rid of that slave woman and her son" (v. 10).
		God speaks
		Listen to Sarah; Abraham's offspring will be through Isaac; both sons will be blessed (vv. 12–13).
LISTENS	**Abraham listens**	**Abraham listens**
	"Abraham agreed to what Sarah said" (v. 2).	Abraham sends Hagar and Ishmael away (v. 14).
SEES	**Hagar sees**	**Ishmael [sees]**
	"I [Sarah] was despised in her [Hagar's] sight" (v. 5).	Ishmael mocks Isaac (v. 9).
	Sarah sees	**Sarah sees**
	"Do to [Hagar] what is good in your sight" (v. 6).	Sarah witnesses the mocking of her son Isaac by Ishmael (v. 9).
	WILDERNESS	**WILDERNESS**

God's Response

SPEAKS	Angel of God speaks	Angel of God speaks
	The angel questions Hagar (v. 8).	"God has heard the boy crying. . . . I will make him into a great nation" (v. 17).
LISTENS	Ishmael named	God listens
	"God hears" (v. 11).	"God has heard the boy crying" (v. 17).
SEES	Hagar names God	God enables sight
	"the God who sees [me]" (v. 13).	"God opened [Hagar's] eyes and she saw a well of water" (v. 19).

The Universal Nature of God's Mission

While the Genesis text records the unfolding fulfillment of God's blessing upon Abraham and his descendants, the Hagar narrative holds a message that is of equal importance—the fulfillment of God's blessing of all creation.[22] Simply put, in choosing Abraham, God does not lose sight of humanity; God's choosing Abraham is, in fact, for the sake of all humanity. Through God's revelatory presence and the promise of blessing to Hagar and her son, Ishmael, the universal nature of God's mission is again made evident. The similarity of God's proclamation of blessing upon creation (Gen 1:28), Abraham (12:3), Hagar (16:10), Ishmael (21:13, 20), and Isaac (26:3) is not coincidental but instead reflects the universal scope of God's missional intentions. As the angel of God announces God's commitment to bless Hagar, the angel states, "I [God] will increase your descendants so much that they will be too numerous to count" (16:10). In Genesis 15:5, God gave a similar promise to Abraham, declaring: "Look up at the sky and count the stars—if indeed you can count them. . . . So shall your offspring be." This literary parallel is not arbitrary, but deliberate; "the author's purpose in so linking these blessings is to connect them to the primeval blessing promised to all humanity: 'Be fruitful and increase in number; fill the land' (1:28). The focus of the Abrahamic blessing is on 'all peoples on earth' (12:3)."[23] As such, Hagar and Ishmael serve as representatives of the peoples of the world. The fulfillment of God's promise upon Abraham, "all peoples on earth will be blessed through you" (Gen 1:3), begins to be fulfilled during Abraham's lifetime, not according to Abraham's will but through the sovereign power and compassion of the Creator God.

---

[22] God repeatedly blesses his creation in the opening sequence of Genesis with fruitfulness and additionally, in the case of human beings, with dominion and resources. God blesses every living creature (Gen 1:21–22), humanity (1:27–29; 5:1–2), and Noah and his offspring (9:1–7).

[23] Sailhamer, *Genesis-Leviticus*, 177.

The universal nature of God's mission is also evident in God's active engagement with individuals from divergent social, religious, economic, political, and cultural spheres. In the Hagar narrative, for instance, God demonstrates his lovingkindness and compassion toward a woman and her son who are both powerless and cast out of society. Claus Westermann explains:

> In the instruction to Abraham, God gives Sarah her way; but the outcast experiences a miraculous deliverance. Sarah has achieved her purpose, but Hagar's story is told for centuries and centuries. It is narrated that God heard the cry of the child who was dying of thirst; he is only the "son of the maidservant," but God has given ear to him. The old story wants to narrate that there is no doing away with the harshness and cruelty of mankind, whereas the merciful God does not abandon the outcasts but lets them experience God's miraculous deliverance.[24]

Knowing Hagar's sociocultural and religious history, it is significant that Hagar, a foreign slave of the lowest social status, becomes a significant figure in the history of Israel. Hagar reflects the "upside-down" nature of the coming kingdom of God,[25] in which the good news is proclaimed to the poor, freedom of prisoners is announced, and the oppressed are set free (Isa 61:1, 2; Lk 4:18).

CONCLUSION

As I reflect on Mary's story, which was introduced at the beginning of this chapter, I remember Hagar's encounters with "the God who sees" (Gen 16:13). While acts of injustice are present in every generation, so is the omnipresent lovingkindness of God. Hagar serves as a witness—both during her lifetime and

---

[24] Westermann, *Genesis 12–36*, 344.

[25] See Donald B. Kraybill, *The Upside-Down Kingdom* (Waterloo, Canada: Herald Press, 2003).

for posterity—of God's covenantal promise to bless all peoples. While God called and blessed Abraham and his descendants, the narrative of Hagar emphasizes that God has not forgotten the rest of humankind. In God's blessing of Hagar and her son, Ishmael, God remembers his original declaration of blessing upon creation and humanity. Hagar and her son become recipients and representatives of the unfolding blessing of God upon the nations. Hagar's encounters with "the God who sees" reveal a theological insight into the character and purpose of God. God's provision for a young slave woman outside of the lineage of Abraham is noteworthy. While humanity is plagued with prejudice and bias, God does not discriminate based on gender, age, wealth, power, or religion. The Hagar story emphasizes, both on a micro and a macro level, the missional themes of God's sovereignty over all peoples, God's faithfulness to humanity, and the universal focus of God's mission.

Chapter 3

Egyptian and Midianite Influences on Moses

Paul Hertig

The intercultural and interfaith experiences of Moses were vast and varied. The encounters explored in this chapter, derived from Exodus, focus largely on Moses's early life: his flight to Midian; his marriage to a Midianite, Zipporah; and his relationship with his Midianite father-in-law, Jethro.

In one sense, every encounter for Moses was intercultural. Though born a Hebrew, he was raised an Egyptian, fled to Midian, and, even when he returned to Egypt to deliver the Hebrews, he was a far cry from an Egyptian or a Hebrew, since he had lived in Midian for forty years (Acts 7:29–30). Having grown up with his future enemies, Moses's Egyptian background prepares him to communicate and negotiate with Pharaoh, in whose household he grew up. Moses becomes the broker between Egypt and the Israelites. But the foundation for Moses's intercultural encounters were laid by Joseph.

MOSES AND JOSEPH: INTERCULTURAL PARALLELS

The context of this study begins with a transition from Joseph in Genesis to Moses in Exodus:

Then a new king, to whom Joseph meant nothing, came to power in Egypt. "Look," he said to his people, "the Israelites have become far too numerous for us. Come, we must deal shrewdly with them or they will become even more numerous and, if war breaks out, will join our enemies, fight against us and leave the country." So they put slave masters over them to oppress them with forced labor, and they built Pithom and Rameses as store cities for Pharaoh. But the more they were oppressed, the more they multiplied and spread; so the Egyptians came to dread the Israelites. (Ex 1:9–12)

Exodus is set in the context of a conflict between two groups of people. The pharaoh of Egypt realizes that the Hebrews, who have become numerous and powerful, might take up arms against Egypt and start an insurrection. He responds to the Israelites in fear, reducing them to slaves. But, of course, the pharaoh's fear that the Israelites will escape does indeed one day become a reality.

Initial intercultural dynamics surrounding the story of Moses are based on power, fear, and a perceived threat. There is nothing healthy about these undercurrents, which will reap only misfortune. Ironically, the system that Joseph, the earlier immigrant, had put in place—the storage of grain in order to survive in times of drought, once appreciated by the Israelites ("You have saved our lives. . . . We will be servants to Pharaoh"—Gen 47:25)—is now a basis for slavery. The "oppressed" slaves are forced to build storage cities for Pharaoh (Ex 1:11). Joseph's system, introduced as a kind gesture from outside for the well-being of Egypt and the surrounding nations, is now corrupted as a form of power over another nation rather than its original intention as a service to the nations. A transcultural arrangement based on generosity, kindness, trust, and reciprocity has gone awry because Pharaoh chooses to no longer trust the Israelites, and now fears them instead.

There are other important connections between Moses and Joseph, two immigrants to Egypt who had intense childhood experiences. Moses follows in Joseph's footsteps as an early prototypical cross-cultural servant of God: Joseph is rescued from a pit of death by non-Israelites, and Moses is rescued from the threat of drowning by non-Israelites; Midianites deliver Joseph, and Pharaoh's daughter delivers Moses. Each one settles in neighboring countries—Joseph in Egypt, and Moses in Midian. Moses and Joseph marry daughters of priests in the country of their migration, and each one fathers two sons. Joseph outsmarts the wise men of Egypt; Moses outperforms the wise men of Egypt.[1]

BABY MOSES'S INITIAL ENCOUNTER WITH EGYPTIANS

As the narrative torch is passed from Joseph in Genesis to Moses in Exodus, intercultural issues pervade the latter's life and situation. Setting the stage, we first glimpse Moses as a three-month-old baby floating down the river in a basket, released by his Hebrew mother, drifting toward the arms of his Egyptian mother. Moving from one culture to another depicts marginality. Moses has a culturally complex destination from birth. His new mother, Pharaoh's daughter, participates in the divine plan as a prototype of God's response to Israel: "I have heard them crying out because of their slave drivers, and I am concerned about their suffering. So I have come down to rescue them" (Ex 3:7–8). She went down, saw the child, heard the cry, took pity, drew him out, and immediately began to provide for his needs (2:5–10). And the princess knows his ethnicity. She explicitly states, "This is one of the Hebrew babies" (2:6). Fully aware of and fully willing to overcome cross-cultural boundaries, and ready to defy her father's political order to throw every Hebrew boy into the Nile, she becomes an early key player in the divine plan to save and empower Moses. Even earlier, Moses's mother had hidden him for three months, defying Pharaoh's edict, but complied subversively by placing him in the Nile, as ordered, within a tiny vessel.[2]

---

[1] Victor P. Hamilton, *Exodus: An Exegetical Commentary* (Grand Rapids, MI: Baker, 2005), 24.

[2] Karen Strand Winslow, *Early Jewish and Christian Memories of Moses' Wives: Exogamist Marriage and Ethnic Identity* (Lewiston, NY:

Thus, Moses's story begins with an Egyptian "enemy" (Pharaoh's daughter) rescuing him from childhood death. "Basic values such as compassion, justice, and courage" are "present among God's creatures quite apart from their relationship to Israel."[3] The participation of non-Israelites in God's plan lays the foundation for God's redemptive activity in which

> there is no difference in effect of the humanitarian efforts of those who fear God and those who do not. Both Hebrew midwives and Egyptian princess are agents of life and blessing. . . . God is able to make use of the gifts of both, and the community of faith is equally accepting of their efforts.[4]

Therefore, while Israelites will be mandated to act justly in an unjust world, many outside of this community will participate in acts of justice with comparable outcomes, prompted by the divine plan, though through differing motives.[5]

Specifically, and more dramatically, the intercultural activity of Pharaoh's daughter parallels the activity of God, providing a precursor to Israel's liberation from Egypt. Just as Moses was drawn out of the water, rescued from the death sentence of Pharaoh, and given provision by Pharaoh's daughter, so Moses will draw out the Hebrews from Egypt and live up to the name given him by the princess. Moses ("one who draws out") will liberate and provide sustenance for the Hebrews.[6] The name Moses early on indicates his dual cultural identity: the name particle *mešu* appears in the names of the Egyptian kings Ahmose and Thutmose, and thus signifies Moses's royal upbringing; the name's nuance of "rescue from the water" indicates his Hebrew heritage and may prophetically refer to his role as the rescuer of the Hebrews from slavery.

Edwin Mellen Press, 2005), 24.

[3] Terence E. Fretheim, *Exodus: Interpretation: A Bible Commentary for Teaching and Preaching* (Louisville, KY: Westminster John Knox Press, 1991), 39.

[4] Ibid.

[5] Ibid.

[6] Ibid., 40; Hamilton, *Exodus,* 23.

In the succeeding intercultural encounter Moses's sister offers a Hebrew woman to nurse her brother, and the royal princess of the Egyptian palace accepts the advice of this Hebrew slave child (2:7–8). "This princess is depicted as a pawn in the sister's hands and in the larger drama scripted by the narrator who is also discreetly sketching a divine deliverer hovering backstage."[7] Shrewdly, Moses's sister, Miriam, conducts a business arrangement for Moses's own mother to be paid from Pharaoh's budget to nurse her own child (2:9—a foretaste of the plundering of Egyptians, 3:22). The double irony is that the princess allows a Hebrew baby boy, given the death sentence by her father, to survive and prosper, paving the way for this child to become the leader and liberator of Israel from Pharaoh's enslavement.

Women are exemplars of those willing to break free from cultural, religious, and political restraints. It matters not whose side these women are on (Egyptian or Israelite). They do what is right in the face of death and injustice. "All five women [the Hebrew midwives, Moses's mother, Pharaoh's daughter, her slave, and Miriam] are actively engaged on the side of life against a ruler who has shown himself to be capable of considerable brutality. Bucking a male-dominated system, they risk their lives for the sake of life."[8] Women are truly givers of life and guardians of life. The compassion and courage of Hebrew and Egyptian women laid the foundation for the Hebrew's deliverance. The multicultural upbringing also lays the foundation for Moses's multicultural calling. Raised an Egyptian, Moses was nursed by his Hebrew mother's milk, yet he will leave both cultures behind for forty years, settling and marrying into a third culture in Midian. These influences become vital for his ability to carry forth his God-given responsibilities in the midst of complex cultures and religions.

Moses' Egyptian household—the household of Pharaoh himself—became his life preserver until he was grown. Thus, each caring and/or cunning female in the story moved the

---

[7] Winslow, *Early Jewish and Christian Memories of Moses' Wives*, 25.
[8] Fretheim, *Exodus Interpretation*, 39.

threatened male infant farther from slave space, where males were endangered, to Pharaoh's space, where (Egyptian) males were safe.[9]

In preparation for his intercultural calling, in which he will identify with the people of his birth and deliver them from oppression, Moses will embody what will be the story of Israel, when he (1) initiates a conflict with the Egyptians (2:11–12), (2) becomes the recipient of Pharaoh's murderous plots (2:15; 1:22), (3) escapes ("flees," 14:5) Egypt to the wilderness and encounters God at Mount Sinai, and (4) describes himself as a sojourner in a foreign land. Therefore, Moses, Egyptian in identity (2:19), must depart from Egypt geographically culturally, and spiritually, to truly identify with the Israelites, and in particular with their suffering, sojourning, and way of life. In the wilderness he discovers a new identity—and so it will be for Israel as well.[10]

MOSES CHANGES SIDES

While we do not know the motivations or context, sometime after growing up Moses goes to "his own people" and "watches them at their hard labor" (2:11a). Immediately, the narrator hints that Moses has begun to identify with the Hebrews, indicating a personal transition from Egyptian affinity to the identification of the Hebrews as "his own people." He then specifically observes an Egyptian beating a Hebrew, again, "one of his own people" (2:11b). The narrator emphasizes this shift in Moses's cultural identity, and this identification is immediately backed by action: "Looking this way and that and seeing no one, he killed the Egyptian and hid him in the sand" (2:12). It is one thing to identify with a particular cultural group; it is a much deeper commitment to defend the group through a particular action. Clearly, Moses,

---

[9] Winslow, *Early Jewish and Christian Memories of Moses' Wives*, 24.

[10] Fretheim, *Exodus Interpretation*, 42.

motivated by a shift in cultural identification, is also motivated by a sense of justice, as indicated by his question in the subsequent verse: "The next day he went out and saw two Hebrews fighting. He asked the one in the wrong, 'Why are you hitting your fellow Hebrew?'" (2:13).

The immediate response of the Hebrew men connotes Moses's status as a stranger to his own people. They counter with a question of their own: "Who made you ruler and judge over us?" (2:14). Ironically, Moses will, one day, become ruler and judge, but he must begin at the point of pain, having already been labeled as an "other" by Egyptian caretakers shortly after birth (2:6). He has killed an Egyptian in order to defend his own people, yet he is still not one of them because he is not a slave like them. "They resent his high-handed interference in their affairs, and perhaps fear being punished for his crime," thus they snap at him; "Moses is now alone, cut off from Egyptian hospitality and his own people alike" with only one option, to escape to a region beyond Pharaoh's control.[11]

Without warning, Moses's attitudes and actions are met with great dissonance; suddenly, he has violently put a man to death in seeking to identify with the people of his birth. He has spoken up for justice, but in his mind, as he flees both his Hebrew and Egyptian origins, he likely feels like a complete failure and a man without cultural belonging. Moses's flight will take him to Midian, where he is introduced to a third cultural identity that ushers in a new spiritual beginning.

> Only among his own people and later in the land of Midian (v. 15) could Moses really become familiar with the God who is the liberator of the captives and the helper of the afflicted, the God of the desert and of the valley of death. Therefore, Moses went out to the Israelite slaves, yet not merely to inspect them or the world outside his own refined

---

[11] John I. Durham, *Exodus: Word Biblical Commentary,* vol. 3 (Waco, TX: Word Books, 1987), 19.

life. What happened to him was a personal exodus that led him to a discovery from which there was no return.[12]

Indeed, Moses had to face his own people first, experience the rejection that they experienced, and then move across the desert for a cross-cultural experience in Midian that would prepare him for yet another cross-cultural experience among his own people in Egypt. Yes, this was a personal exodus of discovery, the beginning of a journey of no return, metaphorically. Moses had risked everything for others. His journey of "no return" thus begins with rejection by the people for whom he sticks his neck out to defend, and also by Pharaoh, who seeks to kill him once again. Moses's action on behalf of the weak sets up the potential for acting on behalf of the weak again. It is important that Moses not only "intervenes on behalf of the oppressed, but even more that he identifies the oppressed as *his people*."[13] This is both a shift in personal values and a shift in cultural identification.

MOSES THE EGYPTIAN BECOMES A MIDIANITE

Moses, now a fugitive in the desert, meets up with seven Midianite sisters at a well. Midian was the son of Abraham, and the younger half-brother of Isaac, and therefore distant kin; the Midianites were longtime nomads.[14] Exodus does not allude to this relationship through Abraham but develops the narrative on the assumption that the Midianites are not of Israel.[15] Midianites are allies to Israel in Exodus and Numbers but enemies to Israel

---

[12] Göran Larsson, *Bound for Freedom: The Book of Exodus in Jewish and Christian Traditions* (Peabody, MA: Hendrickson Publishers, 1999), 23.

[13] George W. Coats, *The Moses Tradition* (Sheffield, UK: Sheffield Academic Press, 1992), 107.

[14] Martin Noth, *Exodus, a Commentary* (London: SCM Press, 1962), 31; Durham, *Exodus*, 20.

[15] Winslow, *Early Jewish and Christian Memories of Moses' Wives*, 20. There is both continuity and discontinuity in the historic relationship

in Numbers and Judges. The Midianites also invaded Palestine periodically. For purposes of this study it is important to note that Moses's encounters with the Midianites are positively nuanced both for Moses and for Israel. Moses's life in Midian is structured so as to convince the audience that "these outsider relations preserved Moses, were essential to his mission, and vital to Israel's early salvation history."[16] Five books later the Bible uses similar language for Midian that parallels Egyptian oppression of the Hebrews: "Midian so impoverished the Israelites that they cried out to the Lord for help" (Judg 6:6). But in the Exodus passage the roles are quite the opposite. The later oppressors are now protectors of the fugitive, Moses. A different context and era, a different experience. The Midianites adopt him into their community, where he is once again nurtured, just as Egyptian oppressors nurtured him in his early life. Cultural patterns and traditions are broken repeatedly in the story of Moses, laying the groundwork for Moses's intercultural and spiritual development.

In fact, Moses's intervention on behalf of the Midianite women at the well is reciprocated when Moses is welcomed into the household of the family of the Midianite women. In contrast to his treatment by the Israelite community, Moses receives several crucial affirmations from the Midianites:

> Moses is not welcome in the Israelite community, but here Moses is shown considerable hospitality by strangers. . . . Israel does not appreciate his acts of justice on its behalf; the Midianites welcome it. Israelites engage in accusations of Moses; the daughters of Reuel publicly sing his praises. Those who stand within the community of faith are abusive; those without faith in Israel's God exemplify genuine relationships.[17]

---

between Israelites and Midianites: amiable (Ex 2:15—3:1; 4:18–19) and hostile (Num 31:1–54; Josh 13:21, Judg 6—8) (Hamilton, *Exodus*, 34).

[16] Winslow, *Early Jewish and Christian Memories of Moses' Wives*, 6, 19–21.

[17] Fretheim, *Exodus Interpretation*, 44.

Therefore, preparing for the unfolding drama of Moses, Yahweh utilizes those outside the community of Israel to affirm, implement, and accomplish Yahweh's ongoing plan for Moses and the eventual exodus. Even while friends and cultural kin are hostile to Moses and run him out of town, the non-Hebrew enemy becomes friend, rescuer, and liberator at key points to move the drama forward.

The five women who acted justly and courageously by intervening to save and nurture Moses have influenced his moral development. This is evident, for example, when he protects and rescues strangers at a well—the seven daughters of Jethro, who were driven away by shepherds (Ex 2:16–17). This marks the second formative moment when Moses takes a stand and acts on behalf of people who have been treated unjustly. Just a few verses earlier in the narrative he struck and killed an Egyptian who assaulted a Hebrew. In that situation he not only addressed an injustice but in the process he "changed sides" during the conflict and identified with the Hebrew rather than the Egyptian. In the case of Jethro's daughters, Moses takes sides based on unjust treatment, regardless of cultural or religious background. He is "clearly cast as a rescuer."[18] The gospel message here is that we must never accept injustice at any level of life, at any time, even if that goes against the established cultural norms or practices.

Interestingly, the Midianite women identify Moses as "an Egyptian" (Ex 2:19). Though he identified himself with the Hebrews prior to fleeing from Egypt, he carried with him some remnants of his Egyptian heritage, observed by the daughters, suggesting that "Moses is at a liminal moment of his life, moving to a new identity."[19] The text clearly establishes this as a cross-cultural situation: when the Midianite women refer to Moses, not by name, but as an Egyptian; and when Moses names his first child Gershom, meaning "I have become an alien in a foreign land" (2:22). "Moses has definitely not forgotten whence he came, and

---

[18] Walter Brueggemann, "Exodus," *The New Interpreter's Bible*, vol. 1, ed. Leander E. Keck et al. (Nashville, TN: Abingdon Press, 1994), 703.
[19] Ibid., 704.

he is not ashamed of his origins. Instead he identifies totally with the suffering of his people."[20]

This concept of knowing one's roots, letting go of one's roots, and starting anew is best summarized in Hebrews: "By faith Moses, when he had grown up, refused to be known as the son of Pharaoh's daughter. He chose to be mistreated along with the people of God rather than to enjoy the fleeting pleasures of sin" (Heb 11:24–25). "Moses's powerful [though unnecessarily violent] intervention on behalf of a Hebrew slave has transformed him from a well-situated member of Pharaoh's household to a fugitive. . . . He is a hunted, unwelcome man. He has indeed become an alien in his own land."[21] Moses, sheltered by a new cultural community, classifies himself as a stranger. This stranger status anticipates a time when he will no longer be a stranger but will return to his own people. Midian, just like Moses's other homelands, is not permanent but transitory. This is indicated in an earlier scripture that begins with the naming of Moses's son and flows directly into God hearing the cry of the Egyptians:

> Zipporah gave birth to a son, and Moses named him Gershom, saying, "I have become a foreigner in a foreign land." During that long period, the king of Egypt died. The Israelites groaned in their slavery and cried out, and their cry for help because of their slavery went up to God. (Ex 2:22–23)

Moses's alien status anticipates his return migration to his own people, who had originally cast him out of their community.

To return to the story of Reuel (Jethro), he is surprised that his daughters left this man (Moses) behind and tells them to invite him to "eat bread," a sign of appreciation, hospitality, and solidarity. The offer of hospitality evolves into a permanent fellowship of breaking bread and to Moses's adoption into the family through the Midianite priest giving him his daughter's hand in marriage. "The hospitality provides not only shelter from the pursuit of

---

[20] Larsson, *Bound for Freedom*, 22.
[21] Brueggemann, "Exodus," 704.

Pharaoh who wanted to kill him, but also the intimacy of a family."[22] Moses then begins forty years of immersion in this third culture, so that he now has three cultural experiences: Hebrew, Egyptian, and Midianite. This includes triple religious influences. The Hebrew and Midianite religious experiences of Moses will be fully established by the end of this chapter. Regarding Egyptian religious experiences, since culture and religion were interwoven in the ancient Near East, "all the wisdom of the Egyptians" that nurtured Moses would have included religion: "Moses was educated in all the wisdom of the Egyptians and was powerful in speech and action" (Acts 7:22).

THE WILDERNESS REVELATION

After establishing the cultural backgrounds of Moses, Yahweh's revelation comes to Moses. God first reveals: "I am the God of your father. I am the God of Abraham. I am the God of Isaac. And I am the God of Jacob" (Ex 3:6). Foundational to any human experience one must know one's cultural roots. Moses has become Egyptian and Midianite but now must return to the culture of his birth, and understand the plight of his people.

As a triple-culture, triple-religious person, Moses is not confined to a parochial view of culture or of God. Moses can follow Yahweh when others cannot because he is not confined or constrained by one particular cultural or religious understanding. However, Moses's statement to Yahweh, "Who am I that I should go to Pharaoh and bring the Israelites out of Egypt?" may very well be more than a statement of doubt and insecurity. Moses mentions two groups—Israelites and Egyptians—in his statement of doubt. This may indicate a lack of cultural and religious belonging. Furthermore, Who am I? is a basic question often posed by those who have more than one cultural identity. Yahweh's answer to Moses's "Who am I?" is "I will be with you" (3:12). The "I am,"

---

[22] Coats, *The Moses Tradition,* 106.

who is always present ("I am who I am," 3:14), doubly assures this presence. "Now go; I will help you speak and will teach you what to say" (4:12). The assurance of the presence of God will be enough to overcome Moses's inadequacy and lack of cultural and religious moorings. Furthermore, Moses's birth brother, Aaron, appointed as comrade in the enterprise (4:14), serves to overcome language and cultural barriers while legitimizing Moses through Aaron's heritage as a Levite and his participation with the enslaved and afflicted Hebrew community. The refrain of God teaming up insider and outsider pervades the Moses accounts.

In retrospect, Moses's new calling sprang from Moses's earlier formative moment when he "changed sides," watched "his own people" at hard labor, and advocated for a Hebrew slave beaten by an Egyptian (2:11–12). Abandoning his royal Egyptian upbringing, he identified with his birth culture and became a fugitive. This new fugitive identity, not an end in itself, served as a transition to a new calling that would dramatically alter his universe at the burning bush. There, God's self-revelation culminates during Moses's journey to the far side of the wilderness (3:1), not in the courts of the Egyptian nobility. As Moses once did, God, too, expresses affiliation with the plight of the Hebrews, stating: "I have seen my people suffer in Egypt. I have heard them cry out because of their slave drivers. I am concerned about their suffering" (3:7). God is both the God of persons—Abraham, Isaac, Jacob, and Moses— and the God of people—the community of enslaved Hebrews in Egypt. Overall, Moses has shifted from pomp to purpose in his new identification with the Hebrew community.

It is not ironic that Yahweh's self-revelation to Moses occurs in the wilderness, and while Moses is tending sheep (3:1). "This shepherd of the sheep identifies with his people so that their suffering, their cry for redemption is his cry."[23] God has advanced Moses's new commitment into a calling. Moses not only identifies with the suffering of the Hebrews, he "embraces the task for doing something about their plight . . . to liberate the oppressed from

---

[23] Ibid., 112.

their oppression."[24] Moses will fulfill his God-given responsibilities in spite of great obstacles and opposition ahead.

ZIPPORAH'S INTERFAITH EXPERIENCE WITH MOSES

The brief, bizarre, and baffling passage of Exodus 4:24–26 is not set in time, or space, or even within its narrative context;[25] thus its inclusion likely indicates its importance. The implied backdrop is a serious and unresolved issue between Moses and God, who attempts to "kill" Moses. Apparently, Moses's failure to circumcise his son results in an impending death sentence.[26] But once Zipporah takes her son's circumcision into her own hands, Moses is absolved. Raised an Egyptian and now a Midianite, "Moses was guilty of not carrying out circumcision in his own family, yet he was the one who was to lead the circumcised nation of Israel from Egypt to the Promised Land. The situation was simply intolerable."[27]

In Zipporah's other two scenes she is silent and obedient: (1) Her father gives her to Moses as his wife, and she bears a son (2:21–22); and (2) her father brings her and her sons to Moses after the exodus (18:1–5). But in this middle scene (4:25–26) she takes quick and decisive action during Yahweh's death grip on Moses. "The Midianite Zipporah thus joins Hebrew and Egyptian

---

[24] Ibid.

[25] Brueggemann, "Exodus," 718.

[26] In reference to 4:24, "If He truly wished to kill Moses, could He not have done so in a moment? . . . He held Moses in a death grip, but He did not want to kill him. The verb 'to seek' means not a frenetic activity on God's part, but a sudden struggle, a divine grip, and divine patience before the final blow. Indeed, He was giving Moses one last chance to stay alive. Strangely, but surely, this is another instance of God's grace. Moses had committed a serious offense against the Lord that made him unfit to be God's agent of deliverance or to live in God's presence." Ronald B. Allen, "The Bloody Bridegroom in Exodus 4:24–26," *Bibliotheca Sacra* 153 (July–September 1996): 265. After the circumcision Allen translates that Yahweh "released" him, that is, from the death grip (ibid., 267).

[27] Ibid., 266.

women who helped him [Moses] survive numerous threats on his life in the early chapters of Israel's birth story."[28] In this case Zipporah delivers Moses from death, allowing the unfolding plot of the "vulnerable hero"[29] to become the deliverer of Israel. Although the passage is obscure, it states that upon circumcision of her son, she then touched "his" legs/feet, a biblical euphemism for genitals (Is 6:2; 7:20).[30] Since she had already touched her son's genitals with the flint, the implication is that she touches Moses with the blood of her son. Then she announces that he is her "bridegroom of blood," and Moses gains another identity, now in a blood bond with his wife, safe from the threat of Yahweh.[31]

By touching Moses and stating that he is now a blood relative, Zipporah transmitted her son's circumcision to Moses as well, making him more than a marriage partner; that is, he is also related through the bond of a blood ritual.[32] Possibly Moses, raised as an Egyptian, agitated God due to his own uncircumcision. Among some Semites the father-in-law circumcised the bridegroom. The Hebrew term for "father-in-law" means "one who circumcises."[33] Possibly, then, Zipporah has taken upon herself the role of her father.

One cannot help but connect other passages in which blood preserves life, such as the smearing of blood on the doorposts and beams during the Passover (Ex 12:22) and Moses's throwing blood on the people to seal the national covenant (24:8). If Moses throwing blood upon people is a parallel, then, "the sealing of the relationship between God and Moses may be in view here. The mediation of Zipporah is then parallel to the mediation of

---

[28] Winslow, *Early Jewish and Christian Memories of Moses' Wives*, 26.

[29] Ibid., 27.

[30] Jonathan Kirsch, *Moses: A Life* (New York: Ballantine Books, 1998), 131; Harold W. Attridge, *The HarperCollins Study Bible—Old Testament* (San Francisco: HarperSanFrancisco, 1993), 86.

[31] Brueggemann, "Exodus," 718. Zipporah's phrase is, literally, "Surely you are a bridegroom of blood to me."

[32] Winslow, *Early Jewish and Christian Memories of Moses' Wives*, 52.

[33] Attridge, *The HarperCollins Study Bible—Old Testament*, 86.

Moses."[34] The ritual blood spilled from the circumcision serves to shield the divine wrath.

Zipporah, the "circumciser and savior," is now a "relative of blood" to Moses; her husband's blood united her with him in a way normally indicative of male bonding.[35] "The bloody circumcision saved the blood-smeared Moses from death, and it bound Moses to Zipporah in a relationship normally reserved for males.[36] Taking this a step further, Zipporah's "quick fix" circumcision, which makes Moses her "blood bridegroom," places the whole family within the covenant of Israel. Moses has gained a new identity, in blood bond with his wife; Zipporah has also gained a new identity, bonded through an Israelite blood ritual. In one fell swoop she and her family convert to Judaism. Indeed, Charles W. Stewart observes, "Religious conversion can be a means of creatively coping with, particularly, the interpersonal stress in one's environment and a healthy problem-solving activity."[37]

Karen Strand Winslow connects the Zipporah narrative to Moses's birth account, in which women save vulnerable males: "A Midianite woman thus became part of the biblical pattern of unlikely, unexpected, marginalized figures, including women and outsiders who acted as saviors of individuals and families significant to the survival of the collective Israel."[38] The interfaith significance of this non-Israelite's bold action deserves further explanation. Zipporah is the only person in this passage who takes action, in word and deed. Considering God's intent, her words and action involve great risk to her own life, yet she is fully aware

---

[34] Fretheim, *Exodus Interpretation,* 79.

[35] Winslow, *Early Jewish and Christian Memories of Moses' Wives,* 21, 34.

[36] Ibid., 54. Winslow postulates that the Zipporah account speaks to a context in Israel when "foreign" wives created controversy. In this case a foreign wife without blood relations becomes bound to Moses through a circumcision rite (ibid., 36).

[37] Charles W. Stewart, "The Religious Experience of Two Adolescent Girls," *Pastoral Psychology* 17 (1966): 55.

[38] Winslow, *Early Jewish and Christian Memories of Moses' Wives,* 54.

of what she needs to do to save Moses and his son. This sets her above the other women who play roles in Moses's early life:

> The difference between Zipporah and the other women is that, while they saved Moses from Pharaoh, she saves him/ his son from God—here the parallel works best with Moses. She thus plays the role of mediator between God and Moses, anticipating the very role that Moses will later play on Israel's behalf. . . . As Zipporah saves Moses from the wrath of God, so Moses will save Israel. . . . However much Moses reaches heroic stature in his later activity, he himself is shown here, right before he embarks on his mission, to be vulnerable and in need of a mediator in his relationship with God. And it is a non-Israelite woman who provides that mediation, saving Moses from sure death.[39]

Zipporah, the Midianite, is thus depicted and remembered as a decisive heroine, skilled entrepreneur, and preserver of the divine plan for Moses and Israel. Zipporah's intervention during Yahweh's death grip further develops the Exodus 1—2 pericope that depicts the dependence of Moses upon "cunning/quick-witted female relatives and compassionate strangers."[40] Therefore, the narrator intersects Midianites, specifically Zipporah and her father, with Moses's mother and sister, Pharaoh's servant and daughter, and the midwives, as collaborators with Yahweh in safeguarding Moses, who will one day deliver the Hebrews from slavery. Hebrew, Egyptian, and now Midianite women were critical in Moses's survival prior to his birth, during his infancy, and on into adulthood in preparation for his mission to deliver God's people from Egypt. Zipporah's circumcision of her son crowns "a pattern in which the un-endangered females in Moses' story-world thwart deadly attacks on endangered males."[41]

---

[39] Fretheim, *Exodus Interpretation*, 80–81.
[40] Winslow, *Early Jewish and Christian Memories of Moses' Wives*, 21.
[41] Ibid., 21, 24.

The interfaith significance of this episode cannot be overstated. A Gentile woman has married into the Israelite line and, through a key decision and quick action, saves and empowers Moses as he is about to embark on his mission to deliver the Hebrews from Egypt. A foreign woman intervenes on behalf of Moses, who already has direct access to God (for example, at the burning bush), and performs an Israelite blood ritual that is traditionally done male-to-male, on behalf of her son and husband, in order to save them from the wrath of Yahweh. Through the process she boldly declares herself now within the bloodline of Moses, a daughter of Israel. Moses's family becomes qualified to become members of the house of Israel as a result of the intervention of Zipporah, a non-Israelite woman.

MOSES'S RETURN TO MIDIAN (EX 18:1–27)

Prior to the reunion of Moses and his Midianite family the narrator pauses to provide a glimpse of the inner life of Moses in a most unusual way—by reciting the names of his sons. Gershom, meaning "I have become an alien in a foreign land" (18:3), expresses cross-cultural dissonance and helplessness, which is healthy for Moses to acknowledge. It recalls Moses's banishment from the "good life" in Pharaoh's court after taking a stand against the enslavement of his own people. Next, the narrator invokes the name of his second son, Eliezer, "help," saying, "My father's God was my helper; he saved me from the sword of Pharaoh" (18:4). This first mention of Eliezer indicates a movement from helplessness to healing. Bicultural, and all the more, tricultural people tend to go through a phase of identity crisis and eventually a phase of identity rediscovery, in which acceptance of a multicultural role may be viewed as positive.

The names of Moses's sons metaphorically depict both Moses and Israel. Both are "alien" and both are "helped" by God. Thus, Moses personally experiences the life of Israel prior to returning to Egypt, where he and Israel will be aliens who are helped by Yahweh. Moses's intercultural preparation is ideal.

It is also important to extend the application of this text to broader contexts, since any community of faith is alien to its culture and depends on its help from God, who both enters into cultural contexts (3:7) and helps the people of faith who are aliens within their cultural contexts (3:8), freeing them to worship the true God (3:12). Therefore, the term *alien* reminds the people of faith not to cozy up to any cultural contexts, as Moses exemplified in choosing not to identify with Egypt, and the term *help* reminds the people of faith that they are neither self-dependent nor alone.[42] Further examples of Moses's reliance on others follows.

JETHRO'S INFLUENCE ON MOSES

Jethro is referred to as the father-in-law of Moses thirteen times and as a priest only once, in 18:1–12. The early emphasis in the meeting of Jethro and Moses is the reunion of Moses's family, specifically Zipporah (18:2–6), explaining that the family had been separated and that Jethro had sent word to him: "I, your father-in-law Jethro, am coming to you with your wife and her two sons" (18:6). Also emphasized is Yahweh's deliverance of Israel from Egypt, which is mentioned five times. Terence E. Fretheim connects these emphases, observing that Moses's family is integrated into Israel's identity as the newly delivered faith community.[43] The initial duty of Jethro is to reunite the separated family after an exasperating phase of separation. It is likely that the sons of Zipporah and Moses were sent back to Jethro after the family had set out for Egypt (4:20), possibly after the terrifying incident when the newly circumcised son may not have been fit for further travel, and/or perceived danger lay ahead for the family. Moses may be likened to a person who must painfully leave family behind when summoned to a military assignment.[44]

---

[42] Brueggemann, "Exodus," 825.

[43] Fretheim, *Exodus Interpretation*, 195.

[44] Hamilton, *Exodus*, 27.

While meeting with Jethro, Moses "declares" to his father-in-law "about everything the Lord had done to Pharaoh and the Egyptians for Israel's sake and about all the hardships they had met along the way and how the Lord had saved them" (Ex 18:8). This is the first report of the biblical fulfillment that Pharaoh had been "raised up" to show "my power and that my name might be declared in all the earth" (9:16). Moses declares the great news of God's powerful deliverance, and Jethro rejoices.[45] Jethro's "use of much of Moses' own language testifies to the basic way in which faith is transmitted from generation to generation" (Deut 26:5–11; Josh 24:2–13)[46] and, in this case, we will now see, from religion to religion.

Upon Moses's declaration of the great wonders of Yahweh, Jethro believes in the God of the exodus community. "Now I know that the Lord is greater than all other gods. See what he did to those who looked down on Israel" (Ex 18:11). Jethro receives the news with conviction and models the "way in which biblical faith is heard and embraced by those once removed from the events (cf. John 20:29)."[47] Moses passes on his faith, for the first time, to an individual and a community. "His witness serves to establish the exodus faith for the first time in a non-Israelite community,"[48] and we discover how an outsider becomes incorporated into the community. Moses has set the example for how the Israelites are called to respond to those outside of their community (see Pss 96:3–4; 67:4). The good news of God's deeds in Moses's testimony sets the tone for the narrative and solicits Jethro's words and actions, as Jethro responds with joy and hospitality. The offerings and sacrifices, and a liturgical doxology, signal celebration and allegiance. Through cross-cultural initiation rites, "Zipporah

---

[45] The same dynamic, though with a different verb, is found in Isaiah 52:7, in which a "messenger" in exile brings good news: "How beautiful on the mountains are the feet of those who bring good news, who proclaim peace, who bring good tidings, who proclaim salvation, who say to Zion, 'Your God reigns!'" (Brueggemann, "Exodus," 826).

[46] Fretheim, *Exodus Interpretation,* 196.

[47] Brueggemann, "Exodus," 826.

[48] Fretheim, *Exodus Interpretation,* 197.

and her father represent a household that originated outside of genealogical boundaries but became allied to Israel through marriage, circumcision, recognition of the Lord's might, and sacrifice/communal meal."[49]

While we do not know the details of the tent discussion, the two emerged and "Jethro, priest of Midian, not Moses, the chosen emissary of Yahweh, or Aaron, the high priest of Israel . . . performed the Bible's first recorded ritual of sacrifice to Yahweh in the wilderness of Sinai . . . blood was spilled on the altar" and when flesh "burned as an offering to Yahweh, it was a pagan who presided over the sacred event. Indeed, Moses is not mentioned at all."[50] Jethro had just declared that he now knows that Yahweh is greater than all other gods, yet one would not expect that confession immediately to qualify him to preside over this sacred ritual, unless Yahweh was somehow honoring his background and experience as priest of Midian. One understands how astonishing this is in comparison to one who meets Christ for the first time, such as the Samaritan woman, and on that very day, declares to her community that this person could be the Messiah (Jn 4:29). There is an astounding reciprocity in Moses's declaration of the wonders of Yahweh, Jethro's declaration of his belief in the supremacy of Yahweh, and then Jethro's leading a sacred ritual of worship. Apparently, the Midianites were skilled at the spiritual rituals of blood sacrifice, evidenced in Jethro's sacrificial offering and Zipporah's circumcision.

Following this celebration comes a reminder that the release of the community from slavery in Egypt does not resolve all problems for all time. People delivered from the structures of oppression must develop healthy and helpful social structures of their own. Such structures require community empowerment and careful implementation. In this case Moses had taken the entire judicial burden on himself, necessitating the intervention of an outsider's warning and advice: "The next day Moses took his seat to serve as judge for the people, and they stood around him from morning

---

[49] Winslow, *Early Jewish and Christian Memories of Moses' Wives*, 72.
[50] Kirsch, *Moses, a Life*, 232.

till evening" (18:13). Jethro's advice first begins with a series of questions (18:14), challenging Moses to reflect on his behavior, asking *what* he is doing and *why* he is doing it. As a cultural outsider who did not participate in the exodus, Jethro's questions demonstrate intercultural humility and communication skills. While the text does not provide the full dialogue, Jethro warns Moses that he and the people coming to him will burn themselves out. He then lays out an administrative plan for the selection and delegation of capable, trustworthy, God-fearing leaders who are not seeking dishonest gain (18:19–23). The meting out of justice becomes a shared responsibility in the community.

Most fascinating is Jethro's interfaith comment that "God [*Elohim*] so commands this" (18:23). While no such known command of God exists, though it might come from his own religious tradition, Jethro has confidence that this administrative plan of shared leadership is in harmony with God's design. Here we find a transcultural truth: "Wise discernment of what seems prudent in this situation is believed to be just as much the will of God as a specific divine verbal communication."[51] Moses's humble response indicates his ability to accept hospitality and advice from those of other cultures and religious backgrounds, in spite of his status as a heroic deliverer. Moses's humility (Num 12:3) contrasts with "great persons . . . [who are] often reluctant to share power."[52] Moses successfully puts the plan into practice, Jethro returns home, and we do not hear from Jethro again in Exodus, even though he has honed Moses's leadership skills and transformed the community.

Practical ideas and methods incorporated by the community of faith that do not come from special revelation might still be closely connected to God's purposes. Individually and collectively, the community of God "should accept its common dependence upon general human experience in the world for much of what they do, recognizing that God the creator has been powerfully at

---

[51] Fretheim, *Exodus Interpretation*, 199.
[52] Larsson, *Bound for Freedom*, 125.

work in the interests of the well-being of all."[53] In other words, the experiences, wisdom, common sense, and creativity of "outsiders" like Jethro can be beneficial for the faith community.

In summary, "Jethro hears, visits the community of faith, rejoices, gives thanks, confesses, presents an offering, and worships. All of this activity is permeated with specific language regarding God's deliverance of Israel."[54] Thus, these responses of Jethro indicate his integration into the faith of the delivered community. This does not necessarily mean that Jethro was unfamiliar with Yahweh, but that he now recognizes, through the stories of Israel's deliverance, Yahweh's greatness in all the earth and power over all, and he integrates his own religious insight into that epiphany. "Jethro recognizes that this community, now constituted as an exodus community, is a new reality in the world, and he wishes to be associated with it."[55]

Jonathan Kirsch points out another angle of this episode: two tribal leaders, mindful of an Egyptian threat, engage in a strategic alliance in order to live in peace in Sinai and Canaan, and the two chieftains seal the treaty with the ancient diplomatic ritual of marriage. This explains Jethro's position of honor and his daughter's secondary role in the formal reunion of Jethro and Moses in which a political fugitive receives refuge in a foreign land through the guardianship of a national leader.[56] Later, they seal it again, through this sacrificial offering. Both of these sealed treaties are initiated by Jethro.

At the heart of the mystery of Jethro is a plain and poignant truth that is conveyed in the biblical narrative. Jethro alone befriended Moses at his moment of greatest need; he harbored the fugitive from Pharaoh's justice for forty years; he betrothed his eldest daughter to Moses and welcomed

---

[53] Fretheim, *Exodus Interpretation*, 200.

[54] Ibid., 196.

[55] Ibid., 197.

[56] Kirsch, *Moses, a Life*, 235.

the Israelite into his clan; he joined in the ritual of animal sacrifice by which Yahweh preferred to be worshipped; and he tutored Moses in the art of governing a nomadic tribe on the move through the wilderness.[57]

Moses's family is integrated into Israel's identity as the newly delivered faith community. Furthermore, Moses's forty formative years in the wilderness prepared him to navigate his way through the wilderness as Israel's shepherd, and Jethro and Zipporah co-collaborated through formative transitions all along the way.

THE MIXED MULTITUDE AND THE NATIONS

We conclude by stepping back from the trees to the forest, from specific interreligious and intercultural encounters, to the multifaceted community of the exodus. A "mixed multitude" (12:38), referring to those who are not descendants of Abraham, accompany Israel out of Egypt. The Passover shifts the story to show that escaping the plague "required choice and cultic participation," indicating that this "universal requirement at the very least opens the rite to non-Israelites," eliminating "absolute distinction between Egyptians and Israelites that dominated the older story."[58] This blurring of national boundaries is represented by the mixed multitude that intermingles Egyptians and Israelites as co-participants in the exodus. The narrative of the community of faith is no longer a national story, but "Passover underscores that the plague of death would not discriminate in an absolute fashion between groups."[59]

In summary, the Passover, together with the mixed multitude of the exodus, the wilderness setting, and the intercultural encounters of Moses in Midian, all set the stage for the universalizing of the

---

[57] Ibid., 235.

[58] Thomas B. Dozeman, *God at War: Power in the Exodus Tradition* (Oxford: Oxford University Press, 1996), 69.

[59] Ibid., 70.

community of Yahweh. Mandates are added to assure inclusivity and the incorporation of non-Israelites into the community. For instance, "Do not oppress a foreigner; you yourselves know how it feels to be foreigners, because you were foreigners in Egypt" (23:10). The Israelites are commanded to reflect on who they once were, as foreigners in Egypt, and look ahead to a community that incorporates foreigners in their midst. "Out of the divided tribes a united nation will emerge. A nation will be born to a new life."[60] Not only will a divided nation unite, but it will be inclusive of foreigners:

> Now if you obey me fully and keep my covenant, then out of all nations you will be my treasured possession. Although the whole earth is mine, you will be for me a kingdom of priests and a holy nation. These are the words you are to speak to the Israelites. (Ex 19:5–6)

The prophets pick up both themes—Israel as a united kingdom of priests and responsible to all nations:

> It is too small a thing for you to be my servant to restore the tribes of Jacob and bring back those of Israel I have kept. I will also make you a light for the Gentiles that my salvation may reach to the ends of the earth. (Is 49:6)

BREAKING THE BOUNDARIES
FROM THE OUTSIDE IN

The broad sweep of boundary-breaking, inside-out themes covered in Exodus include:

1. the courage and common sense of Hebrew and Egyptian women who defy the king's orders, including their own cultural and religious restraints, and instead follow their sense of justice to preserve the baby Moses in the face of grave danger;

---

[60] Larsson, *Bound for Freedom*, 81.

2. Yahweh's culturally specific revelation to Moses (the God of Abraham, Isaac, and Jacob) at the burning bush while shepherding his flock at the far side of the wilderness, in which God speaks directly to him, calling him, in the midst of his cultural and spiritual inadequacies, to deliver the suffering Hebrew community from Egypt;

3. Zipporah's circumcision of Moses's son while Moses is in Yahweh's death grip, and the spilling of the blood that identifies Moses as Zipporah's "bridegroom of blood" that incorporates the family into the Israelite community prior to Moses's return to his own people;

4. Gentile Jethro's ritual sacrifice to Yahweh "near the mountain of God" where the ten commandments are given (18:5), with Moses and family present, in celebration of the exodus and Jethro's own declaration of faith;

5. practical advice on leadership principles incorporated from Jethro, the Midianite priest, "as God so commands" for the Israelite community in the wake of their miraculous deliverance from Egypt;

6. the advancement from a particular community to an inclusive and universal community that incorporates foreigners in its midst and that reaches out to foreigners beyond its community to individuals (18:8–11), even to all nations (19:5–6). The community's relationship with Yahweh places Israel in relationship with the surrounding nations, since Yahweh is the God of all nations.

Within this sweeping narrative, there is an ebb and flow of the spectacular and the ordinary, a continuity of God's intervention and human common experience that readily crosses cultural and religious boundaries. This lays the foundation for the next phase of the book of Exodus, in which the law and covenant are introduced, and the community learns to incorporate strangers and foreigners in its midst (Ex 19ff., specifically, 23:10).[61]

---

[61] Fretheim, *Exodus Interpretation,* 200.

CONTEMPORARY APPLICATION

For a world religions class I assign students to choose a particular religious community to study, enter that setting, attend events, and interview several members of that religious community. Like Moses, these students were surprised by their encounters. Hana Leuze, one of these students, states in her study of a Los Angeles Sikh community:

> It stood out to me that everyone we interacted with was able to quote Jesus to us or contextualize their unfamiliar religion into our Western Christian understanding. It reminded me of the way that Americans who travel typically expect everyone to speak English and accommodate them, instead of taking the time to educate themselves about the local language and culture. Why don't I learn to speak the "language" of other religions, and come to them on their terms before expecting them to explain themselves to me?

Jethro declared that he "now knows that Yahweh is greater than all other gods," and then presides over a sacrifice to Yahweh. Zipporah knows exactly what to do to pacify God's anger during a crisis moment and conducts the sacred ritual of circumcision, even though she is an outsider to the religion. Hana makes a good point: just as those outside of our religion understand our language and rituals, we should be able to have a contextual understanding of other religions.

Chapter 4

Philistine Migration: Biblical Case Studies of Non-Israelite Migrants as God's Missionaries

Robert L. Gallagher

Currently we are living in an era of global upheaval due to widespread migration.[1] We are witnessing the highest levels of human displacement on record, according to the 2018 annual report on global issues by the United Nations High Commission for Refugees. There are an unprecedented 68.5 million forcibly displaced people worldwide. Among them are nearly 25.4 million refugees (over half of whom are under the age of 18, with 57 percent coming from South Sudan, Afghanistan, and Syria), 40 million internally displaced people, and 3.1 million asylum

---

[1] For an overview of the migration issue, see Khalid Koser, *International Migration: A Very Short Introduction* (Oxford: Oxford University Press, 2007); Todd M. Johnson and Gina A. Bellofatto, "Migration, Religious Diasporas, and Religious Diversity: A Global Survey," *Mission Studies* 29, no. 1 (2012): 3–22, who show how the global movement of peoples shapes religious diversity through a number of key issues such as globalization and secularization; and Todd M. Johnson and Gina A. Bellofatto, "Key Findings of Christianity in Its Global Context, 1970–2020," *International Bulletin of Missionary Research* 37, no. 3 (2013): 157–64.

seekers. In addition, there are an estimated 10 million stateless people. Often, governments have denied these people a nationality and access to basic rights such as education, healthcare, employment, and freedom of movement. The report underscores that the refugee crisis has reached the highest level in human history.[2]

Stories of migration are not new. In the Hebrew scriptures the themes of migration and intercultural encounter play a significant role in the outworking of God's mission.[3] The first section of the chapter establishes the biblical view of migration. This provides a platform from which to examine the missional landscape of the books of Samuel before considering three instances of Philistine migration to Israel in the time of David—Obed-edom (the keeper of the Ark); the Cherethites and Pelethites (the bodyguard of the king); and Ittai the Gittite (the servant of the king)—that demonstrate the instrumental role that resident aliens played in salvation history.[4] The final section draws on the missional principles of the Philistine case studies to show how the union between migration and mission expresses itself in lessons for today's world.

BIBLICAL VIEW OF MIGRATION

The global statistics of migration in our contemporary world cause us to ask the question: What are God's objectives in the

---

[2] United Nations, "Report of the United Nations High Commissioner for Refugees: Part I: Covering the Period 1 July 2017–30 June 2018," supp. no. 12 (A/73/12) (New York: United Nations, 17 August 2018), 1.

[3] In this chapter I accept the wider definition of *mission* as "the total undertaking that God has set the church upon for the salvation of the world." The end result of mission is God, through the church, reaching across barriers of culture, language, geography, ideology, and ethnicity to bring people to the kingdom of Christ by announcing the gospel in speech and social action. In addition, for my approach to biblical interpretation, see Paul Hertig, "The Nature of the Reader," in *Mission in Acts: Ancient Narratives in Contemporary Context*, ed. Robert L. Gallagher and Paul Hertig, American Society of Missiology Series, no. 34 (Maryknoll, NY: Orbis Books, 2004), 13–16.

[4] A Gittite is an inhabitant of Gath (see 2 Sam 21:19; 1 Chron 20:5).

midst of such distress and turmoil? Scripture is peppered with the plight of migrants throughout human history, beginning with the expulsion of Adam and Eve from the Garden of Eden; then to King David, whom Saul forces to reside in the Philistine city of Gath[5] as a political refugee; and so forth.[6] In the First Testament the Hebrew word *gêr* was used to describe a variety of people— the alien, foreigner, sojourner, and stranger—and was recorded ninety-two times, with the majority of occasions found in the Pentateuch. The word *gêr* could best be translated as "guest," which by implication spoke of a "foreigner" or "resident alien," and had its linguistic roots in the concept of a sojourner turning aside from traveling on the road to seek lodging as a guest.[7]

God is continuously reaching out to the stranger.[8] With Israel's exodus from Egypt and the subsequent giving of the Law, God presented an occasion for the "mixed multitude who also went up with them [Israel]" (Ex 12:38) to follow the living God. In the Pentateuchal law, God provided an opportunity for the *gêr* of Egypt to participate in the community, together with other peoples

---

[5] The city of Gath in Philistia is the hometown of the giant Goliath and his family (cf. 2 Sam 21:18–22; 1 Chron 20:4–8). On the Canaanite cultural–Philistine political duality of biblical Gath, see Hanna E. Kassis, "Gath and the Structure of the 'Philistine' Society," *Journal of Biblical Literature* 84, no. 3 (1985): 259–71.

[6] For a consideration of the biblical perspective of diaspora mission, particularly the patriarchal narratives of Genesis and Israel's Law, see M. Daniel Carroll R., "Biblical Perspectives on Migration and Mission: Contributions from the Old Testament," *Mission Studies* 30, no. 1 (2013): 9–26.

[7] James Chukwuma Okoye, *Israel and the Nations: A Mission Theology of the Old Testament*, American Society of Missiology Series, no. 39 (Maryknoll, NY: Orbis Books, 2006), 155–56.

[8] Cf. Christopher J. H. Wright, *The Mission of God: Unlocking the Bible's Grand Narrative* (Downers Grove, IL: InterVarsity Press, 2006), 159, 422. For the Lukan view of God reaching out to the stranger with salvation, see Robert L. Gallagher, "Good News for All People: Engaging Luke's Narrative Soteriology of the Nations," in *Contemporary Mission Theology: Engaging the Nations*, ed. Robert L. Gallagher and Paul Hertig, American Society of Missiology Series, no. 53 (Maryknoll, NY: Orbis Books, 2017), 193–202.

that Israel would encounter on its journey.[9] The Bible designates the "stranger" as a non-Israelite residing with God's people. As such, the "stranger" was subject to Israelite law, including the religious decrees. This shows the holistic integration of the *gêr* into the Lord's community. Arie Noordtzij notes:

> In the land of the Lord there could be only one law, viz., that which he had given. This juridical equivalence between alien and native-born was an exception in the ancient world, and in this respect, divine revelation was far ahead of the norms of civilization. It took centuries before aliens were humanly treated, and there are often failures in this regard today.[10]

David I. Smith and Barbara Carvill affirm, "Israel's calling has both an outward and an inward focus. Beyond her borders she is to be a light to the other nations; within her borders she is to be a blessing to strangers, to those from other nations who have taken up residence in her midst."[11]

So far, we have explored the biblical view of migration in the Old Testament from one position; namely, the strangers who leave their homeland and unite with the people of God, such as the Egyptians who joined the exodus, would receive love, compassion, and covenantal endowment proportional to their obedience to Israel's religious laws. Foreign migrants needed to know the Law of God, and live by the Law, to receive the benefits of the Law; in doing so, they experienced the attributes of Yahweh.

There is another facet of migration, however, that likewise contributed to God's salvific purposes. In the scriptures, to augment divine intent, there is evidence of Gentile migration to the

---

[9] See M. Daniel Carroll R., *Christians at the Border: Immigration, the Church, and the Bible* (Grand Rapids, MI: Baker Academic, 2008), 99.

[10] Arie Noordtzij, *Leviticus*, trans. Raymond Togtman, Bible Students Commentary (Grand Rapids, MI: Zondervan, 1982), 249.

[11] David I. Smith and Barbara Carvill, *The Gift of the Stranger: Faith, Hospitality, and Foreign Language* (Grand Rapids, MI: Eerdmans, 2000), 11.

people of Israel through God's sovereignty.[12] In the time of David there were four Philistine tribes who migrated to Israel and were instrumental in securing the reign of David, "a man after the Lord's own heart" (1 Sam 13:14). They are Obed-edom's people, the Cherethites and Pelethites, and Ittai's mercenaries and their families. It is to the migratory Philistines that I now turn my attention to explore the relationship between these resident aliens and the mission of God.[13] In doing so, I seek to answer the following question: During the Davidic monarchy, how did non-Israelite migrants become an ensuing influence in Israel whereby God used them for his messianic intent?[14] I argue that these four non-Israelite clans were crucial in achieving this divine goal. I explain the broader missional landscape of Samuel, in which the case studies take place, before addressing the scriptural evidence supporting this claim.

MISSIONAL LANDSCAPE OF SAMUEL

In considering the background of 1 and 2 Samuel (1100–970 BCE) we need to appreciate that the story focuses on the following:

---

[12] Examples of such movements in which non-Israelite migrants were missionaries include Hagar the Egyptian slave (Gen 16; 21); Jethro the Kenite priest of Midian (Ex 18); Ruth the Moabitess (Ruth 1—4); the Queen of Sheba, the Sabaean monarch (1 Kgs 10); the Roman centurion of the Gospels (Lk 7), and Cornelius, a centurion of the Italian regiment (Acts 10).

[13] For a picture of the Philistines and the cultural milieu in which they lived, see Trude Dothan, "What We Know about the Philistines," *Biblical Archaeology Society* 8, no. 4 (1982): 1–17; this article is based on her book *The Philistines and Their Material Culture* (New Haven, CT: Yale University Press, 1982).

[14] Walter C. Kaiser Jr., *Mission in the Old Testament: Israel as a Light to the Nations* (Grand Rapids, MI: Baker Academic, 2000), 26. Kaiser affirms that it was God's resolve to bless the world by way of David and his dynasty, which was a foreshadowing of the rule of God on earth through the coming Messiah.

Samuel, the last judge (1 Sam 1—7); Samuel and Saul, the first king (1 Sam 8—15); Saul and the rise of David (1 Sam 16—31); and the reign of King David (2 Sam). The emphasis within the narrative is on the start of kingship, kings and their covenant loyalty, the Ark, the Temple and Jerusalem, and the Davidic covenant. The subplots of the books of Samuel, which are a continuation of the Genesis story, are the barren woman (for example, Hannah), choice of the "lesser" (for example, David), leaders and their families (for example, Eli and his sons, Hophni and Phinehas), and intercultural encounters.[15]

One example of the intercultural subplot is the Lord's interaction with the inhabitants of Philistia. God weaves his Person into the cultural tapestry of that nation as the Samuel text recalls the Lord's attributes through narrative and song. This creative strategy portrays the universal power of Israel's God. In times of national crisis the Philistine leaders remembered the deliverance story of the exodus (1 Sam 4:7–9; 6:5–6, 12–16) and the victory song of the Valley of Elah (1 Sam 18:6–9; 21:10–12; 29:1–11) to obtain guidance in their anguish. In this missiological fashion God reaches out to the cities of Philistia to make them aware of his omnipresence. At times, God autonomously intervenes in Philistine history without Israel's involvement (1 Sam 5).[16]

Not all Philistia responded and followed the one, true, living God. There were some clans, however, that did follow. These conditions often occurred through the vehicle of migration, particularly to and from Gath, one of the five cities of Philistia's

---

[15] In Genesis we see the subplots of the barren women (Sarah and Rachel), choice of the "lesser" (Jacob and Joseph), leaders and their families (Abraham, Isaac, and Jacob), and intercultural encounters (Abraham and Isaac with Abimelech the Philistine).

[16] On other occasions God furthered his missional plan through connecting God's people with foreign nations. For example, God revealed his power and presence to the Philistines in Genesis 20; 21; 26; Exodus 13; Joshua 13; Judges 3, 10, 13; and 1 Samuel 4–6, often using the Philistines as his instrument of judgment toward his people (1 Sam 28:19). See 1 Sam 4:7–9; 6:5–6, 12–16.

Pentapolis.[17] For instance, David was in asylum at Gath, and because of his influence, Gittites immigrated to Jerusalem and became a decisive chain in the divine shaping of Israel's history.[18] Carl S. Ehrlich confirms, "One theme which leaps out of the biblical narrative is that of the relationship between Israel and Gath. In the narratives of the united monarchy no other city of the Philistine Pentapolis is mentioned with the importance or frequency of Gath."[19] Indeed, the rapport between Gath and the house of David is striking.[20]

I now examine the association between migration from the region of Gath and mission by reflecting on the following aspects: First, the prestigious position given to Obed-edom the Gittite in the story of the Ark's journey to Jerusalem; second, the amalgamation of the military clans of the Cherethites and Pelethites

---

[17] For a theory regarding the location of Gath and its connections with David, see G. Ernest Wright, "Fresh Evidence for the Philistine Story," *The Biblical Archaeologist* 29, no. 3 (1966): 70–86.

[18] See Robert L. Gallagher, "Coming to Gath: Migration as Mission among the Philistines," in *God's People on the Move: Biblical and Global Perspectives on Migration and Mission*, ed. vanThanh Nguyen and John M. Prior, International Association for Mission Studies Series (Eugene, OR: Pickwick Publications, 2014), 29–45. In addition, see Paul Hertig, "Jesus' Migrations and Liminal Withdrawals in Matthew," in idem, 46–61; and Sarita D. Gallagher, "Abraham on the Move: The Outpouring of God's Blessing through a Migrant," in idem, 3–17. Also see Sarita D. Gallagher, "Blessing on the Move: The Outpouring of God's Blessing through the Migration of Abraham," *Mission Studies* 30, no. 2 (2013): 147–61.

[19] Carl S. Ehrlich, *The Philistines in Transition: A History from ca. 1000–730 BCE* (Leiden: Brill, 1996), 36. For an understanding of the urban development, town planning, and material culture and industry of Philistia, see Seymour Gitin and Trude Dothan, "The Rise and Fall of Ekron of the Philistines: Recent Excavations at an Urban Border Site," *The Biblical Archaeologist* 50, no. 4 (1987): 197–222.

[20] David lived in Gath territory for over a year (1 Sam 27) developing Gittite friendships (2 Sam 6:10–11; 9:18; 15:19–22; 18:2), although later as king making war with Gath (2 Sam 21:18–22; cf. 1 Chron 20:4–8); and finally bringing the region under his sovereignty, and thus subject to Judah (2 Sam 8:1; 1 Chron 18:1; cf. 1 Kgs 2:39–41; 2 Chron 11:8).

as David's royal bodyguard; and last, the integration of Ittai's brigade of Gittite warriors in David's army, and their loyalty to the king during the Absalom rebellion. Each of these Philistine tribal groups had migrated to Israel.

OBED-EDOM: THE KEEPER OF THE ARK

During the reign of Saul, the Ark of the Covenant was lost for twenty years in a Gibeonite town (1 Sam 7:2). The Chronicler accredits Saul's death to the fact that he "did not inquire of the Lord" by using the Ark but relied on a medium (1 Chron 10:14). David's first act as king in Jerusalem was to find the Ark, "for we did not seek it in the days of Saul" (1 Chron 10:13–14; 13:3). After a search party had found the sacred emblem, Levites were transporting the hallowed trophy on a cart from the field of Jaar in Kirjath Jearim when the wagon faltered (1 Sam 7:1–2).[21] When Uzzah, the son of Abinadab, tried to protect the Israelite icon from falling, God killed him (2 Sam 6:3–7). His death was the result of David's disobedience regarding the method of transporting the Ark.[22] David was angry with God and afraid to convey the Ark any farther. The king then left the Ark in the Gibeonite town of Kirjath Jearim, with Obed-edom of Gath, for three months. Moreover, God blessed the Philistine and his family.[23] "And the Lord blessed the family of Obed-edom with all that he had" (1 Chron 13:14). The name Obed-edom indicates that the Gittite migrant farmer was a servant of the gods of Edom. Here is a man who was born in Gath of Philistia (archenemies of Israel), who immigrated to a Gibeonite city belonging to the descendants of

---

[21] See also 1 Chron 13:3, 6; Ps 132:6. The Ark proceeded from Baale of Judah (another name for the Gibeonite town of Qiryath Yearim, the home of Obed-edom [1 Sam 6:21–7:2; 2 Sam 6:2]) to Jerusalem. See Baruch Halpern, *David's Secret Demons: Messiah, Murderer, Traitor, King* (Grand Rapids, MI: Eerdmans, 2001), 291.

[22] See 2 Sam 6:6–11; 1 Chron 13:9–14. Cf. Num 4:15; 7:9; 2 Sam 6:12–19; 1 Chron 15:25–16:3.

[23] See 2 Sam 6:10–11; 1 Chron 13:13–14; 15:25; 26:4–8.

Ammon (for centuries, traditional enemies of God's people), and who lived within Benjaminite tribal territory as a worshiper of the pagan gods of Edom. Yet, with three holy strikes against him, God blessed him.[24]

God's blessing of a Philistine and his family raises a number of questions. Why was a worshiper of Edomite gods a migrant resident in a Gibeonite town instead of living in his native city of Gath? Why was the Ark not left again at an Israelite farm (cf. 1 Sam 6:19–7:2; 2 Sam 6:3)? Why did Obed-edom have the privilege of hosting the Ark of God? Does God's blessing indicate the person's obedience? How did Obed-edom of Qiryath Yearim become David's Gittite ally? The Ark was the dwelling place of "the Lord who is enthroned above the cherubim, where his name is called" (2 Sam 6:2; 1 Chron 13:6). Baruch Halpern concludes, "Plainly, Obed-edom was bound up with the Gittites of David's retinue."[25] I maintain that despite the lack of explanation, this episode demonstrates that through David's disobedience Yahweh blessed a traditional archenemy of Israel with his covenant presence.[26]

---

[24] The blessing of God on humanity is one of the major theological motifs throughout the Old Testament as witnessed in the repetition of Genesis 12:1–3 and involves the goodness of Yahweh in every aspect of a person's life (see Gen 1:22, 28; 2:3; 5:2; 9:1; 18:18; 22:18; 26:4; 27:29; 28:14; Acts 3:25; Gal 3:8).

[25] Halpern, *David's Secret Demons*, 291. Gittites, Gibeonites, and Ammonites were David's main allies in his "civil war" from the south against the House of Saul (2 Sam 2—4). The Gibeonites not only provided the Ark but also David's strategic position in fighting the civil war and the murder of Amasa (2 Sam 20:8).

[26] Mary Evans offers a number of creative scenarios to counter the possibility that even in this emergency, the Bible would entrust the Ark to a Philistine. She asserts, "It may be that Obed-edom was a Levite who had resided for some time in Gath, and was therefore described as a Gittite. Perhaps he was there as part of David's exiled group. It was possible, however, that his family had been long-term resident aliens within Israel, and he, although still known as a Gittite, was a fully accepted member of the Israelite community." Mary Evans, *1 and 2 Samuel*, New International Biblical Commentary (Peabody, MA: Hendrickson Publishers, 2000), 165.

OBED-EDOM'S FAMILY: KEEPERS OF THE ARK

The hand of God's grace and truth upon Obed-edom did not stop when the Levites correctly carried the Ark to Mount Zion. In Jerusalem the Gittite became a gatekeeper of the Ark, and his family of sixty-two men continued to serve God in this worshipful capacity (1 Chron 26:4–8). "God had indeed blessed him" (1 Chron 26:5b). The former polytheistic worshiper from Gath became a son of Yeduthun, one of the guilds of singers at the Temple, and the founder of a clan of Levites.[27] The Levites in this era could include those whom the king commissioned, as with Barzillai's descendants and David's sons (2 Sam 8:18). Obed-edom's family became committed adherents to Yahweh and worshiped the God of the nations. God's abundant blessing of Obed-edom is evidence that God sought to reveal himself spiritually to the Philistines despite their continuing conflicts with Israel (2 Sam 8:1).

A Gittite migrant laborer preserved the most sacred object of God's people. Consequently, Yahweh delivered the consecrated responsibility of maintaining the Ark to his immigrant family.[28] This reflects God's desire for the Philistine people to know and worship God's glory. Halpern highlights the phenomena: "All the

---

[27] 2 Sam 6:10–11. See 1 Chron 13:13–14; 15:18–25, esp. vv. 18, 21; 16:5, 38; 26:4, 8, 15; cf. 2 Chron 25:24.

[28] We find a parallel situation in Jerusalem today. Located in the Old City of Jerusalem is the Church of the Holy Sepulcher, the place most Christians believe is the site of the crucifixion, burial, and resurrection of the Lord Jesus. Dating back to the fourth century the church has attracted Christian pilgrims with its architectural remnants of the Roman Catholics to the icons of the Orthodox churches (Armenian, Coptic, Ethiopian, Greek, and Syrian); it contains the final stations of the Via Dolorosa (the last journey of Jesus to the crucifixion). For more than thirteen hundred years the Nuseibehs, a Muslim family, have been the custodians and doorkeepers of the site of the crucifixion. The Nuseibehs have helped keep the peace between the competing Christian factions since Caliph Omar Ibn Kattab first conquered Jerusalem for the Islamic Empire in 638 (the only gap being the eighty-eight years of Crusader rule in the twelfth century).

signs thus point to a long and sincere Davidic commitment to the Philistines of Gath."[29] The happenings also indicate God's dedication to Gath. The scriptures reveal another case of the Lord's intentions to reconcile the peoples in the region of Gath through David's intersection with the Cherethites and Pelethites.

CHERETHITES AND PELETHITES: THE BODYGUARD OF THE KING

When David and his band of soldiers operated out of the city of Ziklag, some ten miles southwest of Gath, they were in the same region as the Cherethites and Pelethites.[30] The Cherethites, a warrior tribe of Philistines, originated in Crete. Their name in Hebrew means "executioners." In the Bible the Pelethites are always associated with the Cherethites because they were also nomadic inhabitants of the central Negev, the southern section of Canaan.[31] When David and his soldiers were vassal mercenaries

---

[29] Halpern, *David's Secret Demons*, 294; see ibid., 150, 281, 287, 296, 302, 306, 330–31, which support the notion of David's continued allegiance with Gath.

[30] See Eugene H. Peterson, "David at Ziklag," in *Leap over a Wall: Earthy Spirituality for Everyday Christians* (San Francisco, CA: HarperSanFrancisco, 1997), 91–101. For the identification of the geographical site of Ziklag, see Joe D. Seger, "The Location of Biblical Ziklag," *The Biblical Archaeologist* 47, no. 1 (1984): 47–53.

[31] For a mention of "the Negev of the Cherethites," see 1 Samuel 30:14. Also see Joyce G. Baldwin, *1 and 2 Samuel*, Tyndale Old Testament Commentaries (Downers Grove, IL: InterVarsity Press, 1988), 167; and P. Kyle McCarter, Jr., *II Samuel*, The Anchor Bible, vol. 9 (Garden City, NY: Doubleday, 1984), 256, 435. For support of the idea that the Philistines originally came from Crete, and hence also the Cherethites and Pelethites, see Amos 9:7. On the notion of the connection of the Philistines and Cretans, see W. F. Albright, "A Colony of Cretan Mercenaries on the Coast of the Negeb," *The Journal of the Palestine Oriental Society* 1 (1921): 187–94. Evans suggests that one reason why these two groups were so loyal to David was the common enemy of the Amalekites (see 1 Sam 30:1–20, esp. v. 14) (Evans, *1 and 2 Samuel*, 135).

of Achish, king of Gath, they formed a relationship with these two Philistine clans. P. Kyle McCarter, Jr., contends, "The presence later on in King David's army of a contingent of Cherethites, who showed a particular loyalty that continued into Solomon's reign, suggests that David won their allegiance decisively in his days at Ziklag."[32] This would explain David's actions toward the Cherethites and Pelethites once he became king.[33]

When Saul, the Benjaminite, became the first king of united Israel, he made Gibeah the national capital because it was the foremost city of his tribe. He also appointed soldiers of his clan as his bodyguard (1 Sam 22:6–7). Yet, when David became the second king of the united monarchy, God directed him to make Zion, the Jebusite stronghold, the Israelite capital ("My resting place forever"), which incorporated finding the Ark (Ps 132:13–14). He then appointed the Cherethites and Pelethites as his closest guards (2 Sam 8:18).[34]

---

[32] McCarter, *II Samuel*, 435. The Bible reveals Cherethite loyalty continuing into Solomon's reign through the Carite troops in 2 Kings 11:4, 19. Halpern concedes (without substantial explanation), "In the main body of the account of Solomon's reign, in 1 Kings 1–10, the Gittites, Cherethites and Pelethites, and David's 600 men from Gath, disappear" (Halpern, *David's Secret Demons*, 371).

[33] See 1 Sam 30:14; 2 Sam 8:18; 15:18; 20:7, 23; 1 Kgs 1:38, 44; 1 Chron 18:17. The word *Pelethites* is a variant of the term *Philistine* (Arnold A. Anderson, *2 Samuel*, Word Biblical Commentary, vol. 11 [Dallas, TX: Word Books, 1989], 137, 203). Bill T. Arnold states that the Pelethites were professional troops distinct from Israel's regular army (*1 and 2 Samuel*, The NIV Application Commentary [Grand Rapids, MI: Zondervan, 2003], 580). King David used them in initial offensives against the enemy, while he held Israel's regular army in reserve for the final battle. Israel attached these elite troops directly to the king, and they were loyal only to him. Baldwin adds, "By employing foreign guards to ensure the safety of the king, David would minimize the possibility of becoming the victim of inter-tribal rivalries; these men from Crete could give whole-hearted allegiance to him" (*1 and 2 Samuel*, 224).

[34] Benaiah, the son of Jehoiada, a valiant Hebrew soldier (2 Sam 23:20–23; 1 Chron 11:22–25), was in charge of the Philistine protectors of King David throughout his reign. Benaiah's name means, "Yahweh is intelligent."

David chose the enemies of Israel to be his closest protectors, not the soldiers of Judah. Perhaps the sustained situation of David's association with Gath caused Israel to question the king's allegiance to God's people. Indeed, David's refrain to Judah and Israel, "You are my brothers, you are my bone and my flesh," could insinuate such a state of affairs (2 Sam 19:11–15; cf. 2 Sam 5:1).[35]

When David came to power, furthermore, he trusted the two military clans from the region of Gath more than he trusted his own suspicious people. Did David merely buy these two tribes of Philistia for a price, or was their loyalty deeper? Tracing the record of David's Philistine protectors through the scriptures helps answer these questions and reveals a group of Philistine soldiers who were loyal to David and his royal lineage no matter what the predicament. Surely the motivation for their dedication was more than monetary gain. A national crisis during the king's autumn years highlights the uncommon commitment of the Cherethites and Pelethites.[36]

---

[35] The contrary exclamation "We have no share in David, no part in Jesse's son!" (2 Sam 20:1; 1 Kgs 12:16) reflects David's opponents who contended that David was a Philistine agent. Halpern argues, "David's enemies regarded him as a non-Israelite. Specifically, they thought of him as the Gibeonite agent of Philistine masters. They accused him of importing a foreign icon, the ark, as his state symbol. He consistently allied with foreign powers to suppress the Israelites whom he dominated. He spent most of his career as a brigand-king, and, where he ruled, he did so by employing murder and mayhem as tools of state-craft" (*David's Secret Demons*, 479). On the other hand, the Samuel text exonerates David from the charge of collaboration with the Philistines in the war on Saul's house, the civil war (2 Sam 21:15–22).

[36] Another instance of Cherethite and Pelethite loyalty to King David was the second rebellion against David's monarchy by Sheba at the Jordan River (2 Sam 20:7, 23; cf. 2 Sam 8:18; 15:18). This foreign mercenary bodyguard, however, betrayed David at the end of his life by collaborating with Bathsheba (one of his harem women) by installing Solomon (henceforth known as the son, not of David, but of Uriah the Hittite) on the throne instead of his heir, Adonijah (1 Kgs 1:38, 44).

LOYALTY IN THE MIDST OF REBELLION

Israel's prosperity plateaued after David's adultery with Bathsheba and the subsequent murder of her husband, Uriah the Hittite. Never again would the nation enjoy the "justice and righteousness" it had experienced under King David's earlier reign (2 Sam 8:15).[37] Not only did the Israelites suffer the consequences of David's sin but also the sinful ramifications of his family. Similar to Eli and Samuel, David did not challenge his sons in their sin, and thus this affected his relationship with God and Israel. Thus, David lacked godly administration (1 Sam 2:25, 29; 8:3, 5). David took little responsibility for correcting his children and allowed them to determine their own unruly way of living (see 2 Sam 13–15; 1 Kgs 1:6).

The books of Samuel show evidence of David's passive fatherhood in many instances.[38] For example, David's conscious neglect of his family and people enabled Absalom, his third son, to sway the hearts of Israel to rebel against God's king (see 2 Sam 15:6; cf. Ps 3:1–8). Absalom first secured the rebellion in Hebron, his father's city. In quick succession the treason swept across Judah to the other tribes of Israel. In a span of only a few hours David learns of the betrayal of his beloved son, city, tribe, and nation. His once prosperous kingdom collapses. As he made his way out of Jerusalem in funeral procession, he heard of the treason of Ahithophel, his most intimate confidant, and Mephibosheth,

---

[37] See Eugene H. Peterson, *First and Second Samuel*, Westminster Bible Companion (Louisville, KY: John Knox Press, 1999), 171–72.

[38] Richard Nelson notes that the writer of Kings moved from outside the palace to inside the palace in an effort to show how David's passivity signaled the time for some sort of change to take place—in this case, the crowning of Solomon as God's choice of the next king (1 Kgs 1:6). Nelson contends that David's passivity is "underlined" by three issues in the text: "his inability to get warm, have sex, or control his son" (*First and Second Kings: Interpretation: A Bible Commentary for Teaching and Preaching* [Louisville, KY: John Knox Press, 1987], 17). See 2 Sam 13:21; Ps 51.

his covenant son.[39] It seemed that all of Israel had turned against him—his family, friends, kinfolk, and people.[40]

Yet, in the midst of such despair, David found a loyal people. Three Philistine clans stood by David's side during the most demanding crisis of his political career. These three bands were his Philistine bodyguard (the Cherethites and Pelethites), and the six hundred soldiers from Gath under the command of Ittai the Gittite. Bill T. Arnold, commenting on the rebellion of 2 Samuel 15:17–18, muses, "Ironically, it was foreign troops attached to David personally who prove the most loyal (especially the Cherethites and the Pelethites), and foreigners in the Transjordan who support him in his most desperate hour."[41] David's encounter with the region of Gath is especially significant with respect to the migration of the Cherethites and Pelethites. This again is an indication that God sought to reach the Philistine people despite Israel's reluctance to be a light to the nation of Philistia.[42] In regard to this chapter, the last significant intercultural encounter during this period was between David and Ittai, together with his military brigade from Gath.

---

[39] See Ahithophel, the grandfather of Bathsheba in 2 Samuel 11:3 and 23:34. Cf. 2 Sam 15:12, 31; 16:23. Eliam, Ahithophel's son, was one of the thirty-seven generals in David's army, together with Uriah the Hittite, the husband of Bathsheba (2 Sam 23:34, 39). Cf. 2 Sam 12:11–12; 16:20–22. See Mephibosheth in 2 Sam 16:3. Cf. 1 Sam 9:1–13; 18:1–4; 20:8, 12–17, 42; 23:16–18.

[40] To observe the worshipful humility of David in the center of a national crisis, see 2 Samuel 15:13–16:14. Also see Eugene Peterson, "David and Absalom," in *Leap over a Wall*, 193–204. On an interpretation of David's career in its historical context, see P. Kyle McCarter, Jr., "The Historical David," *Interpretation* 40, no. 2 (1986): 117–29.

[41] Arnold, *1 and 2 Samuel*, 610.

[42] For Israel's calling by God to be "a light of the nations so that the Lord's salvation may reach to the end of the earth," see Isaiah 49:6 and Acts 13:47. God eventually brought an oracle of warning judgment against the Philistines (and the Cherethites) five hundred years after the united monarchy of Israel (Ezek 25:15–17; Zeph 2:4–7).

ITTAI THE GITTITE: THE SERVANT OF THE KING

I have already shown that before David was king of Israel, he lived in the hinterland around Gath and built a trusting relationship with three military tribes (Cherethites, Pelethites, and Gittites).[43] David's immigration to that Philistine city and his subsequent relocation to Ziklag by Achish (the king of Gath) allowed the Hebrew refugee to form a rapport with Ittai and his mercenaries (see 2 Sam 15:19–23; 18:2, 5, 12).[44] Halpern affirms that Ittai, along with six hundred Gittites, had been with David in his days at Ziklag, and that Gath was an independent state, "so that Gittites in the service of the king of Jerusalem were in a foreign land (2 Sam 15:18–22)."[45] At this time, Gath was not a vassal of the Israelite state under compulsion to do service to the

---

[43] David was in Gath for a period of time since he learned to play the gittith, a musical instrument of the region, and used the instrument in composing Psalms 8, 81, and 84 (note the superscript of the Psalms). God gives evidence of his cross-cultural grace by such worship—"How lovely are thy dwelling places, O Lord of hosts! My soul longed and even yearned for the courts of the Lord; my heart and my flesh sing for joy to the living God"—played on a Philistine gittith (Ps 84:1–3).

[44] McCarter, *II Samuel*, at first suggests that according to an early source (labeled "Syr."), the six hundred soldiers in 2 Samuel 15:18–19 were an army raised before David went to Gath (in the earlier narrative episodes), and therefore they were not true Gittites, in the literal sense of the word. This seems rather odd. Does he mean that they were Israelites who moved to Gath with David, and that was why they were "mislabeled" Gittites? Yet McCarter contradicts this thought by maintaining that while David was serving in the army of the king of Gath, he "won the loyalty of this contingent of Gittite mercenaries" (370). I agree with Peterson when he states that the Cherethites and Pelethites were foreign mercenaries, not blood Israelites, and so were under David's personal authority (*First and Second Samuel*, 207–8). I believe that the six hundred Gittites were Philistines who David brought with him to Hebron and Jerusalem from his fugitive period in Ziklag, those years that he was under the patronage of King Achish of Gath.

[45] Halpern, *David's Secret Demons*, 149. Also see, for the alliance between David and the Gittites, ibid., 23–24, 79–80, 281, 287–88, 293–95, 302–3, 326, 371. For an understanding of the covenant relationship

people of God. David's collaboration with Gath allowed him the opportunity to import Philistines to Israel. Hence, six hundred Gittites shadowed him throughout his reign (2 Sam 18:2). This number of soldiers represents a brigade, and it was a significant number, equal to a large national army, let alone the army of a city such as Gath with limited resources.[46]

Ittai's six hundred Gittites made up a garrison unit from the central hill country of Gibeah of the Benjaminites, a town that had been a Philistine stronghold until Saul occupied it (2 Sam 23:29; 1 Chron 11:31).[47] It is no coincidence that the Gibeonites received the Ark from the Philistines, Ittai and Obed-edom the Gittites came from the same region, and David supported the Gibeonites while Saul persecuted them.[48] In sum, "the origin of the alliance between David and the Gibeonites lay in their common collusion with Philistine elements."[49] David's victory in the "civil war" against Israel (2 Sam 2), and later with his son Absalom (2 Sam 15), "owed much to his following of six hundred Gittites led by Ittai" who taught and supported the king in Philistine combat tactics in the lowlands and mountains.[50]

ABSALOM'S CIVIL WAR

When Israel followed Absalom into revolt, the national army marched toward Jerusalem, and the three Philistine tribes (Cherethites, Pelethites, and Gittites) consolidated their fidelity toward

---

between David and Achish of Gath, and the resulting loyalty of the six hundred Gittites, see Kassis, "Gath and 'Philistine' Society," 268–69.

[46] Halpern, *David's Secret Demons*, 152. Cf. 1 Samuel 13:5, where the entire Philistine army is some thirty thousand troops, or approximately six thousand soldiers from each of the five cities of Philistia's Pentapolis (see 1 Sam 6:4, 17–18; Judg 3:3).

[47] Ibid., 153. The garrison was located at "the hill of God" in Benjamin (1 Sam 10:5; 13:3).

[48] 2 Sam 21:1–9. Cf. 1 Kgs 3:4–5; 1 Chron 21:29; 2 Chron 1:3, 13.

[49] Halpern, *David's Secret Demons*, 306.

[50] Ibid., 305.

the king. David's Philistines supported him when most of Israel turned against him. Halpern proclaims, "David knitted together a coalition of non-Israelites against the Israelites whom he ruled."[51] Greatly outnumbered in battle, the Philistines could have returned home to both Gath and the central Negev, or retreated alongside a foreign king with a stolen monarchy. Civil war meant living as fugitives with little likelihood of remuneration. 2 Samuel 15 discloses the evolving crisis in Jerusalem:

> All his [King David's] men marched past him, along with all the Cherethites and Pelethites; and all the six hundred Gittites who had accompanied him from Gath marched before the king. The king said to Ittai the Gittite, "Why should you come along with us? Go back and stay with King Absalom. You are a foreigner, an exile from your homeland. You came only yesterday. And today shall I make you wander about with us, when I do not know where I am going? Go back, and take your people with you. May the Lord show you kindness and faithfulness." But Ittai replied to the king, "As surely as the Lord lives, and as my lord the king lives, wherever my lord the king may be, whether it means life or death, there will your servant be." David said to Ittai, "Go ahead, march on." So Ittai the Gittite marched on with all his men and the families that were with him. (2 Sam 15:18–22)[52]

David's offer to release the Gittites from any obligation was a compassionate gesture. Ittai's reply to David, besides, echoed the

---

[51] Ibid., 292.

[52] In 2 Samuel 15 the narrator repeats the phrase "the king" in verses 3, 6, 7, 9, 15, 16, 17, 18, 19, 21, 23, 25, and 27, which is always stated in the context of David as the king. Thus, I believe that the king mentioned in the New American Standard Bible translation of the passage, "Return and remain with the king," is referring to the king of Gath and not Absalom (2 Sam 15:10), which is contrary to the translation of the New International Version quoted in my essay.

covenantal declaration of other non-Israelites such as Achish to David and Ruth to Naomi (1 Sam 29:6; Ruth 1:15–17).[53]

Joyce G. Baldwin maintains, "From his response, Ittai reveals himself to be a believer, for whom love and faithfulness were paramount."[54] Baldwin's persuasion that the commander of the Gittite forces is a "believer" stems from his oath, "As the Lord lives." Walter Brueggemann likewise declares, "David [was] moved and convinced by the foreigner's [Ittai's] words."[55] The biblical narrator surely witnesses the providential hand of God among the Gentiles, and not just another fortunate turn of events for the king. David's successes were the Lord's own deeds.

Subsequently, David promoted Ittai to a position as one of the three highest-ranking officers in Israel's retreating army, alongside Joab and Abishai, the king's nephews. Perhaps this occurred because of David's public decree of covenantal blessing on the honorable and loyal Gentile commander.[56]

Eugene H. Peterson commends this line of reasoning when he comments:

> Ittai is a bright spot in this dark story. He is a Philistine from Gath, the hometown of the giant Goliath. David made his early mark on Israel's life by killing Philistines; now in his later life one of them, Ittai, joins his company and

---

[53] Peterson discusses the confessional language from the lips of Ittai the Gittite (2 Sam 15:21) (*First and Second Samuel*, 209). For further understanding of the relationship between Ittai and David, see Halpern, *David's Secret Demons*, 289, 305.

[54] Baldwin, *1 and 2 Samuel*, 260.

[55] Walter Brueggemann, *First and Second Samuel: Interpretation: A Bible Commentary for Teaching and Preaching* (Louisville, KY: John Knox Press, 1990), 303.

[56] Compare Ittai (Hebrew: "God is with me") with King David's nephews in 1 Chronicles 18:15; 27:34; 2 Samuel 18:2, 5; also see 2 Samuel 2:18; 1 Chronicles 2:16; 11:20–21; 18:12–13. Halpern concedes, "In the main body of the account of Solomon's reign, in 1 Kings 1–10, the Gittites, Cherethites and Pelethites, and David's 600 men from Gath, disappear" (*David's Secret Demons*, 371).

helps him. Unlike the Cherethites and Pelethites, who were paid to be there, Ittai is there out of personal loyalty, and perhaps spiritual conviction. Was Ittai a convert to David's God? Quite possibly, for theological terms are used in the conversation: David blesses Ittai with God's "steadfast love and faithfulness" (v. 20), and Ittai uses Israel's confessional language ("As the Lord lives"—v. 21) in his response. David started out killing Philistines; he ends up converting them![57]

CONTEMPORARY APPLICATION

At the beginning of this chapter I declared that we are living in a time of unparalleled global people movements and that God is calling the church to be a light to the displaced nations. God commanded the covenantal people of Israel to care for the strangers in their community. Arthur F. Glasser notes that the oppression faced by the Israelites in Egypt "was to serve as a constant reminder that they were not to be exploiters and dehumanizers of persons in the way that Pharaoh's people had treated them. Freedom and justice for all were to be the hallmarks of God's land."[58]

As the Israelites were once slaves of Egypt, we too were once slaves in need of freedom, separated from God's household. As Paul declares in Ephesians, "You are no longer strangers and aliens, but you are fellow citizens with the saints, and are of God's household" (2:19). As the Israelites were to love the *gêr* as a neighbor in remembrance of the exodus, so we ought to love our foreign neighbor out of gratitude for our liberation in Christ. Patrick D. Miller states, "The experience of being slaves and strangers marks forever the way those who have been released and given a home treat those whom they encounter as slaves and

---

[57] Peterson, *First and Second Samuel*, 209. Compare David's marriage dowry for Michal in 1 Samuel 18:22–27 with his later connections with the Philistines of Gath.

[58] Arthur F. Glasser, *Announcing the Kingdom: The Story of God's Mission in the Bible*, ed. Charles E. Van Engen, Dean S. Gilliland, and Shawn B. Redford (Grand Rapids, MI: Baker Academic, 2003), 86.

strangers. Love the Lord and love the stranger—that is indeed the greatest of the commandments."[59]

As the new Israel, the Christian community is similarly obligated to fulfill God's directive to dispense steadfast love to the foreigner in our midst, with the Old Testament Law serving as a model of contemporary diaspora mission (1 Pet 2:9–12). As the Western church inevitably meets refugees, immigrants, and exiles in its own backyard, it should draw these people into a protective community of involvement. These guests need the welcoming kindness of the church, where they can have their immediate societal needs met, and an opportunity to explore the gospel: to choose to accept and become a part of a loving network or move on.

We can equally obtain several missiological lessons for today's world from the three Philistine case studies. In the Samuel text, Philistine intercultural encounters and subsequent allegiance to David establishes a faith in the Lord among certain Philistine tribes. We can see the result of these cross-cultural relationships in the lives of Obed-edom, and the Cherethites and Pelethites who, after immigrating to Israel, God blesses and uses as protectors of the Davidic throne. In particular, Ittai, the Gittite leader, fosters an awareness of the Lord, which God further enriches by the Philistine's migration to Jerusalem in support of David's kingdom. This incident in David's reign provides another example of the connection between migration and mission. In simpler terms, because of migration there developed a cross-cultural relationship between the Israelite king and the aforementioned Philistine clans that has contemporary missiological implications.

The Philistine immigrants to the nation of Israel show that migration played a role in the mission of God. We should give consideration, therefore, to these divine strategies for the church today. Who are the immigrant clans in our neighborhood? Are there people from the nations of Burma, Ethiopia, Iraq, Mexico, and Syria that live in apartment blocks or across the way? Could God use them to bless our Western churches? Are we open to

---

[59] Patrick D. Miller, *Deuteronomy: Interpretation: A Bible Commentary for Teaching and Preaching* (Louisville, KY: John Knox Press, 1990), 127.

receive the unique divine perspective that only the stranger can impart? Alternatively, are we closed to that possibility, and thus only partially receive all that the Lord Jesus desires to share with us?

Who are the Philistines in your region? Why not connect with them and receive God's full blessing as David did with the tribes from the region of Gath?[60]

CONCLUSION

Israel's personal experience as a dislocated people evoked an awareness of the need to demonstrate covenantal love to the stranger. When David conquered Goliath of Gath, he had no idea that in a short time King Saul would estrange him among the archenemies of Israel. Because of the political unrest within Israel, David first immigrated to the city of Gath as a political refugee, and then again as a military leader, allowing him to intermix with the Philistines of that region. Consequently, God's self-revelations to the migrant clans of Obed-edom, the Cherethites and Pelethites, and Ittai influenced the evolving destiny of the inhabitants of the city of Jerusalem and the nation of Israel. Similarly, many in the church, having immigrated to different parts of the world as strangers, should also be mindful of dispensing God's transforming love, as God has loved them.[61]

Whether a Philistine is on the move to Jerusalem or the United States, migratory movements continue as an important dimension of the global spread of the Christian faith to bring about the missional purposes of God, affecting both the people of God and

---

[60] Regarding the proper attitude of Christian believers—Jesus Christ is the unique and decisive revelation of God for the salvation of the world—toward adherents of the world religions, see Lesslie Newbigin, "The Gospel and the Religions," in *Landmark Essays in Mission and World Christianity*, ed. Robert L. Gallagher and Paul Hertig, American Society of Missiology Series, no. 43 (Maryknoll, NY: Orbis Books, 2009), 149–59.

[61] See J. Samuel Escobar, "Mission Fields on the Move," *Christianity Today* 54, no. 3 (2010): 28–31.

society toward a renewed faith. Parker J. Palmer concludes, "The stranger is not simply one who needs us. We need the stranger. We need the stranger if we are to know Christ and serve God, in truth and in love. For it is by knowing the truth and by serving in love that we ourselves will be set free."[62]

---

[62] Parker J. Palmer, *The Company of Strangers: Christians and the Renewal of America's Public Life* (New York: Crossroad, 1994), 65.

Chapter 5

Naomi and Ruth: Displacement, Dislocation, and Redemption

Young Lee Hertig

There are many books and articles on the book of Ruth, and many wedding sermons refer to its compelling story. So why write yet another chapter on it? Because the stories of widows depicted in the book of Ruth are particularly significant today as people face massive displacement and dislocation. The criminalization of asylum seekers extends even to children who are detained without due process. Like the Holy Spirit, people throughout human history have been mobile—on foot and by boats, buses, and planes. The push-and-pull factor of human migration remains consistent in terms of the search for food and a better life, but now the scale of contemporary migration, which is different from the ancient migration from Bethlehem to Moab on foot, poses a critical humanitarian crisis.

One of the challenges of reading the ancient texts through contemporary filters and contexts is that it entails the bridging of multiple hermeneutical horizons. Amid the viral #MeToo movement in an age of disruptive social media, it is tempting to superimpose the sexual norms and mores of today onto the ancients.

Yet the patriarchal system is not limited to the ancient world but persists in different, but similar, shapes and forms today. How women navigate the patriarchal systems then and now merits our attention as we attempt to reimagine the hyper-androcentric context of today.

Issues addressed in this chapter include (1) the globalized neoclassical economic policy and inequality and inequity; (2) border crossing; (3) intergenerational bonding in crisis; and (4) internalized patriarchalism.

NEOCLASSICAL ECONOMIC POLICY AND HUMANITARIAN CRISIS

Like Naomi and Ruth, many refugees and asylum seekers on the southern border of the United States seek basic human needs for survival and experience separation and losses along the way. Indeed, poverty is one of the worst forms of violence and it is also criminalized. Recently, more than twenty-five hundred children at the southern border of the United States have been separated from their parents, including breastfed babies. Countless numbers of migrants walk in the deadly heat of the deserts worldwide, risking their lives.

According to United Nations data from 2017, the number of international migrants, 258 million, continues to increase at an alarming rate. Over 60 percent of migrants live in Asia (80 million) or Europe (78 million). North America hosted the third largest number of migrants (58 million).[1] Like Naomi and Ruth, these refugees search for a sustainable life, at the very least for food and shelter.

Since the main driving factors of migration are economic, we must examine the decades-long dominant economic policy, the neoclassical, which is mired in inequality and inequity. Theologian Sallie McFague tackles the fundamental assumption of neoclassical

---

[1] Department of Economic and Social Affairs, "International Migration Report" (New York: United Nations, 2017), 5.

economic policy woefully and accurately: "Human beings are self-interested individuals who, acting on this basis, will create a syndicate or machine, even a global one, capable of benefiting all eventually. Hence, as long as the economy grows, all individuals in a society will sooner or later participate in prosperity."[2] The value of self-interest rarely translates and trickles down. Instead, self-interest begets greed and more greed, resulting in the unsustainable and dangerous inequality and inequity many people face today. Flawed assumptions and policies stemming from this neoclassical economic policy cascade across almost all systems. Moreover, patriarchal theology is not spared from its overreach, and therefore a search for an alternative theology is urgent. For this reason McFague's alternative vision of planetary theology overcomes the anthropocentric worldview and calls humans to be stewards of all God's creation for mutual sustainability.[3] We would be wise to remember this saying by Charles Birch: "The rich must live more simply, so that the poor may simply live."[4] McFague describes this simplicity as life abundant, not scarcity.

By contrast, we have witnessed an extreme concentration of wealth under the neoclassical economic system. According to Credit Suisse Research Institute's 2017 report, with the increase of global wealth the wealth pyramid also soared: "Total global wealth has now reached USD 280 trillion and is 27 percent higher than a decade ago at the onset of the financial crisis. US gains account for half of global wealth increase. The wealthiest 1% of population own 50.1% of all household wealth in the world."[5] Decades ago, Martin Luther King, Jr.'s, call for restructuring an "edifice" that causes poverty was a prescient warning: "We are called upon to help the discouraged beggars in life's marketplace.

---

[2] Sallie McFague, *Life Abundant: Rethinking Theology and Economy for a Planet in Peril* (Minneapolis, MN: Fortress Press, 2000), 77.

[3] Ibid., 127–32.

[4] Charles Birch, Nairobi World Council of Churches Assembly, Address, 1975.

[5] Credit Suisse Research Institute, "Global Wealth Report: Where Are We Ten Years after the Crisis?" (2017).

But one day we must come to see that an edifice which produced beggars needs restructuring."[6] Compared to King's day, wealth disparities in the United States have increased; now, the three richest Americans hold more wealth than the entire bottom 50 percent of the American population, a total of 160 million people.[7] Such an edifice of wealth largely comprises those who benefit from self-interest. The poor are not present at the policymaking table, yet the victims, such as asylum seekers, are detained and their children caged.

Amid the massive and increasing wealth concentration for the few, we face a dire flipside—a record-breaking number of people (250 million) who are displaced and dislocated. A "zero tolerance" policy, which some have claimed is sanctioned by Romans 13:1–5,[8] sent a shock wave to Americans and triggered the dark side of American slave history, when that same passage was used to justify racism and slavery. In contrast, Pope Francis says that "saving the life of someone fleeing war and poverty is an act of humanity."[9]

CROSSING MULTIPLE BOUNDARIES (DISPLACEMENT AND DISLOCATION: *GÊR* AND *NOKRIYA*)

Naomi and her family—her husband, Elimelech, and their two sons, Mahlon and Kilion—set out for the country of Moab, facing many of the same factors that cause global migration today. They were escaping famine in their hometown, Bethlehem. Boldly, they

---

[6] Martin Luther King, Jr., *A Testament of Hope: The Essential Writings of Martin Luther King, Jr.,* ed. James Washington (New York: Harper and Row, 1986), 250.

[7] Chuck Collins and Josh Hoxie, *Billionaire Bonanza: The Forbes 400 and the Rest of Us* (Washington, DC: Institute for Policy Studies, November 2017), 4.

[8] See, for example, Lincoln Mullen, "The Fight to Define Romans 13," *The Atlantic* (June 15, 2018).

[9] Pope Francis, official Twitter account (June 20, 2018).

entered Moab, historically Israel's enemy because Moab's founding was the result of incest between Lot and his eldest daughter. Despite the Israelites' attitude toward Moab, famine in Bethlehem takes Elimelech and his family to this foreign land. Israel blames the intermarriages between Israelite men and Moabite women for Israel's ensuing idolatry.[10] Two sons of Naomi marry Moabite women: Orpah and Ruth. We can surmise their insurmountable hardships from the fact that all the men in the family died after ten years of displacement and dislocation in Moab, leaving only Naomi and her two Moabite daughters-in-law.

Indeed, crossing multiple boundaries of ethnicity, geography, class, and religion poses enormous challenges to people who risk suffering family deaths. The survivors, widows with no welfare system, find themselves hopeless and helpless. Not only is Naomi mournful, but she is also bitter over the losses that make her feel abandoned by God (Ruth 1:20): "I went away full, but the Lord brought me back empty. Why call me Naomi? The Lord has afflicted me; the Almighty has brought misfortune upon me" (1:21). Naomi's compounded suffering creates a physical, emotional, and theological crisis. She no longer wants to be called Naomi ("pleasantness") but instead calls herself Mara ("bitterness"). The name Mara reminds me of a prevailing Korean collective emotion, *han*: "the collapsed anguish of the heart due to psychosomatic, social, economic, political, and cultural repression and oppression."[11] This unresolvable suffering and pain often linger from generation to generation.

Ruth's determination to accompany Naomi back to Bethlehem results in even more losses: (1) her Judean husband in Moab; (2) her father-in-law, Elimelech; (3) her brother-in-law Kilion; (4) her homeland in Moab; (5) her nationality; (6) her citizenship; (7)

---

[10] Gale A. Yee, "Racial Melancholia and the Book of Ruth," in *The Five Scrolls: Texts@Contexts*, ed. Athalya Brenner-Idan, Gale A. Yee, and Archie C. C. Lee (London: Bloomsbury T & T Clark, 2018), 63.

[11] Andrew Sung Park, *From Han to Healing: A Theology of the Wounded* (Nashville, TN: Abingdon Press, 2004), 11.

her native language; (8) "her people," in order to become part of
Naomi's people; (9) her native deity, probably Chemosh, in favor
of Naomi's God (1:14–16); (10) her sister-in-law Orpah; and
(11) her newborn son, Obed, whom she relinquishes to Naomi
(4:16–17).[12]

Yet Naomi claims her bitterness to be greater, telling her
daughters-in-law: "It is more bitter for me than for you, because
the Lord's hand has gone out against me!" (1:13). Multiple
border crossings and the experience of displacement and dislocation thus elicit overwhelming bitterness, similar to *han*, which
is deeply embedded in the Korean collective psyche. Whereas
Naomi became Mara to express her *han*, Ruth remains silent
about her losses. Going through challenges in one's own hometown is hard enough, but international migration as unwelcome
widows in a strange land poses unimaginable hardships. Under-
standably, Naomi feels abandoned by God, and bitterness fills
her heart and soul.

According to Hebrew biblical scholar Gale A. Yee, the Hebrew
language has two different terms for foreigners: (1) *gêr*, which refers to an emigre who lacks full-fledged membership, but is granted
some protections (Elimelech's crossing the border is referenced
with the term *gêr*); and (2) *nokriya*, which connotes negativity,
and highlights the person's otherness and separateness from the
dominant culture.[13] Ruth refers to herself as *nokriya* in her first
encounter with Boaz, her future husband.[14] In other words, Ruth
understands her Moabite ethnicity as *nokriya*; she feels herself to
be a perpetual foreigner in Judea.

---

[12] Yee, "Racial Melancholia and the Book of Ruth," 63.

[13] Ibid., 127.

[14] Gale A. Yee, "'She Stood In Tears amid the Alien Corn': Ruth, the
Perpetual Foreigner and Model Minority," in *They Were All Together in
One Place? Toward Minority Biblical Criticism*, ed. Randall C. Bailey,
Tat-siong Benny Liew, and Fernando F. Segovia (Atlanta: Society of Bibli-
cal Literature, 2009), 127.

INTERGENERATIONAL AND INTERETHNIC
SOLIDARITY *(JEONG)*

Ruth, the Moabite daughter-in-law, accompanies Naomi back to her hometown, Bethlehem. Unlike her sister-in-law, Orpah, who went back to her home at Naomi's urging, Ruth enters into her deceased husband's hometown, an outsider. The two widows' relationship is translatable to our current contexts, as it describes a beautiful intergenerational and interethnic woman-to-woman relationship that may restore hope amid seemingly insurmountable, darkest moments. The two women's stories in the ancient world still illuminate resilient grace and perseverant hope.

As noted earlier, after ten years in Moab Naomi experiences multiple losses in a foreign land, including her husband and two sons. Multivalent bonding in crisis takes place when Naomi hears the news that God is providing food for her people. The intergenerational, interethnic, and interreligious bonding between this mother-in-law and daughter-in-law is surprising and captivating. Ruth has everything to lose by following Naomi to Bethlehem as a Moabitess and widow, yet she remains determined to follow Naomi, her mother-in-law, whom she respects.

Ruth's speech to Naomi, loaded with indelible affection and loyalty, resembles a composite, sticky-rice-like Korean emotion called *jeong*. It is a difficult concept to translate into English. It encompasses "attachment, bond, affection, or even bondage."[15]

> Don't urge me to leave you or to turn back from you. Where you go I will go, and where you stay I will stay. Your people will be my people and your God my God. Where you die I will die, and there I will be buried. May the Lord deal with me, be it ever so severely, if anything but death separates you and me. (Ruth 1:16–18)

---

[15] Christopher K. Chung and Samson Cho, *The Significance of "Jeong" in Korean Culture and Psychotherapy* (Los Angeles: Harbor-UCLA Medical Center), 1.

Christopher K. Chung and Samson Cho address the location of *jeong* as both inside and outside of our hearts, "between individuals" and yet "collective."[16] In contrast to American individualism, both the Korean *jeong* and Ruth's affectionate bonding with her mother-in-law demonstrate the value and practice of collectivism.

Prerequisites for crossing multiple boundaries include acute self-awareness and self-relinquishment. Because Ruth's self-awareness is deep, she is able not only to relinquish her own desires, but also to cross the most challenging boundaries in order to follow Naomi. As her name indicates, Ruth ("companion") accompanies Naomi in her migratory return to Bethlehem. Though vulnerable, the text does not mention either of them being criminalized. Instead, Naomi and Ruth manage to survive through ancient Near East hospitality and kinship.

NAVIGATING THE PATRIARCHY

In a patrilineal system women are excluded from a safety net when they lose their husbands. In fact, a woman's entire identity is dependent on her father before marriage, her husband after marriage, and her sons in widowhood. Being widowed in this culture, left without husbands and sons, means that she has become a nonbeing. Similarly, Asian kinship robs daughters of their equal share of inheritances and prevents them from participating in the many visible male-centered ritual performances.

In a patriarchal world women have had to be creative in the way they negotiated their survival. For instance, Naomi's instructions to Ruth in how to get access to Boaz are part of an elaborate, step-by-step scheme. During their journey Naomi vows to find Ruth, a Moabitess and widow, another husband, since that is the only survival tactic in a patriarchal culture. Naomi's deep-seated internalized patriarchalism surfaces almost comically when seen through a modern lens, when she urges her daughters-in-law to return to their homes:

---

[16] Ibid.

Am I going to have more sons, who could become your husbands? I am too old to have another husband. Even if I thought there was still hope for me—even if I had a husband tonight and then gave birth to sons—would you wait until they grew up? Would you remain unmarried for them? (Ruth 1:11–13)

Meanwhile, Ruth goes out to the field to "pick up the leftover grain" (2:2), and "as it turned out, she found herself working in a field belonging to Boaz" (2:3). It is unlikely that Ruth ended up at Boaz's field by coincidence, since Boaz was well aware of Ruth and her loving treatment by Naomi. And he responds, "My daughter, listen to me. Don't go and glean in another field and don't go away from here." Boaz's favor of Ruth overwhelms her. She exclaims, "Why have I found such favor in your eyes that you notice me—a foreigner?" (2:10). Boaz's reply to Ruth reveals Naomi's plan to find her a husband:

I've been told all about what you have done for your mother-in-law since the death of your husband—how you left your father and mother and your homeland and came to live with a people you did not know before. May the Lord repay you for what you have done. May you be richly rewarded by the Lord the God of Israel, under whose wings you have come to take refuge. (2:11–12)

Boaz's empathic words and blessing for a refugee like Ruth are lacking in current global and US contexts of migration.

Having lived as a stranger in a strange land in Moab, Naomi chooses to be a matchmaker for Ruth in Bethlehem for her welfare. She assures Ruth another marriage in Bethlehem in order to sustain her in what is to her a foreign land:

My daughter, should I not try to find a home for you, where you will be well provided for? Is not Boaz, with whose servant girls you have been, kinsman of ours? Tonight he will be winnowing barley on the threshing floor. Wash and

perfume yourself, and put on your best clothes. Then go
down to the threshing floor, but don't let him know you
are there until he has finished eating and drinking. When
he lies down, note the place where he is lying. Then go
and uncover his feet and lie down. He will tell you what
to do. (Ruth 3:1–4)

Naomi's instructions are loaded with endearment, *jeong,* which
Ruth demonstrated when she insisted on accompanying Naomi
for her return migration. The only means of survival for widows
like Ruth was marriage. The women's schemes succeed. Boaz again
blesses Ruth and calls her "a woman of noble character" (3:11),
and she becomes Boaz's wife. And Naomi, who is too old to re-
marry, also benefits, because she is able to sell her late husband's
land to Boaz as part of his marriage. Widows are basically treated
as addendums to the deceased man's property when it is sold. "On
the day you buy the land from Naomi and from Ruth the Moabitess, you acquire the dead man's widow, in order to maintain the
name of the dead with his property" (4:5). Obviously, only males
have the right to own land, and their names are preserved even
after they are deceased. However, a widow becomes "part of the
deal" during the real-estate transaction.

A Moabitess and widow, Ruth gets a second chance by marrying a Judean man, Boaz. Many contemporary widowed and
divorced women find fewer prospects for remarriage than their
male counterparts do. How the two widows navigate the patriarchal systems remains significant today in a persistently patriarchal
world. For example, many church women still face a "stained-glass
ceiling." Therefore, when united in navigating obstacles, they may
manage to find male allies.

Ruth enters into the Jewish genealogy by giving birth to a
son, whose own son is Jesse, the father of David. Deborah Hearn
Gin notes that the "widow" is listed in Deuteronomy 16:14 last
in the "biblical caste" category system, after orphans. In addition to the twelve references to Ruth's name, she is depicted as

a "Moabite" six times.[17] Gin resonates with Ruth's multivocal identities and the way she utilizes them in various contexts. For example, regarding Ruth's assertiveness in dealing with Boaz as a foreigner and her self-identification reference to Boaz, Gin states:

> Initially, she referred to herself as Boaz's handmaid *(amah)*. Upon getting his attention, however, she proceeded to speak in a voice more reminiscent of her Moabite roots: "Spread your cloak over your handmaid *(amah)*, for you are next-of-kin" (3:9). Ruth not only followed Naomi's advice; she went beyond Naomi's plan and offered a proposal of marriage to Boaz![18]

Truly remarkable character and courage are revealed in Ruth's actions as she moves from multiple outsider social locations into insider space.

As much as Ruth, an utterly "other," broke into the insider's space, and even into the genealogy, she is still perceived as a foreigner in Bethlehem. Even after she gave birth to a son, the public acknowledgment of her as a mother seemed forbidden. Ruth is even praised for her loving loyalty to Naomi as being better than seven sons (4:15). And then, when Ruth gives birth to a son, the village women say, "Naomi has a son" (4:15–16). Naomi, seen as the mother, not the grandmother, names Ruth's son. Ruth's rightful place as the mother is dislocated.

Ruth is basically "an alien kinswoman" who gave birth to a son whose patriarchal lineage matters; her son becomes the father of Jesse. Yet Ruth had to yield to her mother-in-law, Naomi, an insider who benefits from her kinship, when Ruth gives birth to a son:

---

[17] Deborah Hearn Gin, "Ruth: Identity and Leadership from Multivocal Spaces," in *Mirrored Reflections: Reframing Biblical Characters*, ed. Young Lee Hertig and Chloe Sun (Eugene, OR: Wipf and Stock, 2010), 59.

[18] Ibid., 63.

> Then Naomi took the child in her arms and cared for him. The women living there said, "Naomi has a son!" And they named him Obed. He was the father of Jesse, the father of David. (Ruth 4:15–17)

This happens even after Ruth was elevated as better than seven sons in her care for her mother-in-law! However, even with exclusive kinship and lineage, when a Gentile woman births a son, she is not seen as his mother. This kinship boundary cannot be crossed. God breaks through that cultural taboo, however, and Ruth's name is recorded in the genealogy as the one who gave birth to David's grandfather.

Notable in the story are the changing power dynamics between the two women, as Naomi is now in her homeland and Ruth in a foreign land. During the crisis in Ruth's homeland in Moab, Naomi was as vulnerable as Ruth. However, in Bethlehem, Naomi has access to social capital—her kinship and the inheritance of her husband's land.

Similarly, the Asian Confucian familial system privileges the male child to carry the lineage. Therefore, when a son is born, the mother gains power and credibility. In contrast, the birth of daughters assigns blame to the mother, not the father. Consequently, it is a competitive rather than cooperative relationship that often epitomizes the relationship between the mother-in-law and daughter-in-law. This perpetuates a hierarchical relationship rather than solidarity. Hence, the narrative of Naomi and Ruth illustrates how women under patriarchy can foster a solidarity that debunks the "divide and conquer" myth of the oppressed. The Naomi and Ruth story speaks powerfully to contemporary Asian and Asian American families.

It is unimaginable what it would be like to have to yield a rightful mother's position to a mother-in-law. Moreover, Ruth remains a perpetual foreigner even after giving birth to her son! On the other hand, Joan Chittister commends Naomi and Ruth for demonstrating deep concern for the situation of the other in a hostile world. "Loss changes life at the root," states

Chittister.[19] The losses that these two widows face entail enormous survival challenges with no welfare system, and thus their powerful stories resonate deeply with modern-day slave laborers and refugees. The survival strategies and bonding of Ruth and Naomi in crisis provide ample inspiration for addressing the human crises of today.

All Asian cultures affected by Confucian patriarchalism typically ensure male privilege over females. Favoritism of sons over daughters is pervasive among both men and women. In the case of women, as Naomi and Ruth gain access to power by attaining male allies and birthing a son, similarly, Asian and Asian American mothers gain power for their in-laws when they birth sons. For these reasons I am lifting up the relational dynamics between mothers-in-law and daughters-in-law, and the way they may forge an unlikely solidarity in crisis.

Exceptional in this relationship between Naomi and Ruth is their endearing *jeong*. Naomi, as an older woman, engages in power brokering for her daughter-in-law's welfare. This is similar to the way Esther managed King Xerxes's palace dynamics, although Naomi's situation is less complicated.

As a powerless woman and a widow, Naomi relies on her kinsman, Boaz, for Ruth's sustainability in Bethlehem as a foreigner. Without a patriarch, Ruth, as a widow in a foreign land, has no future. Boaz notices Ruth when she is gleaning grain from his field. Through power brokering and connections, Naomi exemplifies a woman's survival tactics in a patriarchal culture. This patriarchal culture still has a strong hold today, and many women leaders in churches continue to suffer from a lack of job opportunities and pay gaps. A lack of egalitarianism has influenced Christian churches and college campuses all over the United States and remains strong today, and young people in particular are often targeted.

---

[19] Joan Chittister, *The Story of Ruth: Twelve Moments in Every Women's Life* (Grand Rapids, MI: Eerdmans, 2000), 10; see also 1–2.

CONTEMPORARY APPLICATION

Breaking through the gender ceiling today requires power brokering with the male-dominant system and male allies. Breaking through also requires women's solidarity with women. So many women, whether consciously or unconsciously, still operate under male-centered norms and see other women as competitors in their pursuit of advancement. In contrast to this "queen bee" syndrome, Naomi and Ruth exemplify the forging of solidarity with both fellow women and older wise women.

Without such solidarity many widows and orphans today cannot sustain themselves. Yet zero-tolerance policies inflict added pain on poor children and adults who pursue asylum. God weeps with them, and so do we. What collective actions can we Christians take against the persecution of vulnerable immigrants?

I began this chapter discussing refugees, estimated today at 250 million with many more not accounted for. The sheer scale of migration today is not exactly comparable to the ancient migration of Naomi and her family. Nevertheless, the factors of migration in ancient and current times remain the same, as these factors are ubiquitous throughout time and space. Even now, the Holy Spirit migrates and hovers over the universe, waiting for the people of God to arise from their comfortable homes and to love the stranger as Jesus does.

Chapter 6

Mordecai and Esther: Intercultural Negotiations and Power Dynamics

Young Lee Hertig

THE DRAMA OF POWER BANQUETS

Esther, a Jewish queen in a Persian palace, uses the king's tool for exhibiting power, the banquet, to reverse the fate of her people. Similarly, many contemporary banquets engage in power plays by the inclusion or exclusion of guests, by seating some at the head table and not others, and by designating some people to serve and some to be served. As the first minority woman faculty member at a particular seminary, I elicited formal and informal, visible and invisible power dynamics that caused me to question constantly how the leadership of the institution perceived and interpreted my presence and voice. I felt vulnerable in the sense that I was at the mercy of the dominant cultural norms and interpretations, with no point of contact with whom I could clear up misunderstandings. Also, the curriculum mainly focused on Western knowledge and thus lacked diversity in representations, contributions, and perspectives.

More than two decades later I had a chance, as someone now outside the seminary, to bring the underrepresented Asian American voices to the seminary curriculum. To that end I invited key Asian American Christian leaders to a series of meetings with the dean, provosts, and president. I also organized a banquet at which some of these Asian American leaders were speakers, and at which I presented awards to Asian Pacific Islander spiritual leaders to honor their legacies. Moreover, the chef, menu, speakers, award honorees, and topics of the talks were all Asian American. One of the benefits of organizing a series of symposiums and banquets, from the outside in, was that I was able to bypass the internal politics of the institution. What I thus helped to produce was a truly intersectional and alternative third space of learning, apart from regular classroom environments. Notably, as a result, this particular seminary finally founded an Asian American Center and brought this underrepresented community from the outside (and from the margins) to the inside of the institution.

Similarly, although they are initially outsiders of King Xerxes's palace, Mordecai and Esther eventually become insiders. As migrants into the king's palace, they exhibit spirit-filled, cross-cultural power brokering as they befriend the enemy in order to carry out their mission of saving their own people. They manage to reverse the power of the "other"—King Xerxes "changes sides" and empowers Esther and Mordecai through multiple twists and turns in his court. The king reverses Haman's plot when Haman speaks to him about hanging Mordecai on the gallows. Haman enters the court, and the king asks him, "What should be done for the man whom the king delights to honor?" (Est 6:6). Thinking that the king would be honoring Haman himself, Haman suggests that such a person should be paraded through the streets with a royal robe that the king has worn and a horse the king has ridden, one with a royal crest placed on its head (6:7–9). "Go at once," the king commands Haman. "Get the robe and the horse and do just as you have suggested for Mordecai the Jew" (6:10). Thus, a Gentile king affirms the Jewish mission in spite of Haman's plot to slaughter all the Jews.

TWO EXTRAORDINARY QUEENS

The book of Esther depicts two extraordinary queens with similar and unique ploys within the patriarchal palace system. The similarity resides in their "if I perish, I perish" spirit and in their use of banquets to reverse fortunes. Queen Vashti displays overt courage by refusing King Xerxes's summons to show up to the king's banquet (seemingly naked), wearing her royal crown (1:10), during the height of their drinking from goblets of royal wine. Instead, she hosts a separate women's banquet at the palace (1:9). The magnitude of Vashti's actions is demonstrated by the reactions of the king and his officials, and seven lawyers are summoned by the angry king to decide what to do about Vashti's disobedience (1:13–14). They were afraid that the queen's defiant behavior would embolden all the other women in the kingdom, thus endangering the patriarchal system (1:17). To ensure that the patriarchy will continue, the king's edict is proclaimed throughout the Persian Empire: "Every man should be ruler over his own household" (1:22).

One difference between the two extraordinary queens is Vashti's overt defiance in bucking the abusive patriarchal system versus Esther's covert "gaming" of the system. Esther executes a series of schemes, quietly tapping into the king's power in order to thwart an imminent threat of genocide against her people. Esther and Mordecai, two outsiders, deftly navigate the power dynamics inside the Persian palace. A young Jewish girl, Hadassah (Esther) conceals her ethnicity through her cousin Mordecai's coaching (2:20) and succeeds the deposed queen of Persia. The duplicity of her names—Hadassah ("righteousness") and Esther ("hiddenness")—speaks to her internal shrewdness and her external innocence in her engagement with the Gentiles in their court. Her attributes foreshadow the saying "I am sending you out like sheep among wolves. Therefore, be as shrewd as snakes and as innocent as doves" (Mt 10:16).

Since Esther's dual identity requires a "both-and" lens to appreciate fully, I employ a "yinist" epistemology, derived from

Taoism, which sees reality through a both-and holism.[1] Yin, the feminine energy in Taoism, includes the masculine energy, yang. Likewise, yang, the masculine energy, includes the feminine energy, yin. In Jungian psychology the male's unconscious feminine inner archetype is called anima (yin), and the female's counterpart is called animus (yang). Based on the yinist wholeness of being and becoming, I examine the ways in which two outsiders—Mordecai and Esther—utilize yin and yang energy for power brokering within the inner palace. Following Mordecai's coaching, Esther eventually reverses Haman's genocide plot against her people. Mordecai's defiance of paying honor to Haman (3:2) sets an example that parallels Vashti's earlier refusal to honor the king's request. The Persian queen, Vashti, is expelled at sixteen years old, and even more striking, a Jewish girl, only fourteen years old, not only enters the Persian court but also replaces Vashti.

Robert Greene, in his best-selling book *The 48 Laws of Power*, provides historical background on the palace court of the ancient Near East:

> Throughout history, a court has always formed itself around the person in power—king, queen, emperor, leader. The courtiers who filled this court were in an especially delicate position; they had to serve their masters, but if they seemed to fawn, if they curried favor too obviously, the other courtiers around them would notice and would act against them. Attempts to win the master's favor, then, had to be subtle.[2]

That Esther, a Jewish outsider, succeeds Vashti and enters the enemy's palace shows the interplay of yin and yang energy. She executes a complex series of maneuvers that sets up a Shakespearian type of drama. Her mission involves boldness in disguise and

---

[1] For a deeper explanation of this epistemology, see Young Lee Hertig, *The Tao of Asian American Belonging: A Yinist Spirituality* (Maryknoll, NY: Orbis Books, 2019).

[2] Robert Greene, *The 48 Laws of Power* (New York: Penguin Books, 2000), 1.

a savvy scheme of power brokering (yang), resulting in a reversal of the power dynamics in the banquet arena where she carefully wields her power. In other words, Esther manages to use the tool of the king's power display, the banquet, to change the fate of her people. Ten banquets are held in the book of Esther, and they each reveal the arena where the major power brokering takes place:

1. Xerxes's banquet for the nobility (1:2–4)
2. Xerxes's banquet for all the men in Susa (1:5–8)
3. Vashti's banquet for the palace women (1:9)
4. Esther's enthronement banquet (3:15)
5. Haman's and Xerxes's banquet (3:15)
6. Esther's first banquet (5:4–8)
7. Esther's second banquet (7:1–9)
8. The Jews' feasting in celebration of Mordecai's glory and the counter decree (8:17)
9. The first feast of Purim: Adar 14 (9:17, 19)
10. The second feast of Purim: Adar 15 (9:18)[3]

According to Carol M. Bechel, these banquet arenas set power reversals in motion. For example, the Persian feasts (in banquets 1 and 2) contrast with the Purim feasts (9 and 10). The banquet that caused Vashti's demotion as queen (3) contrasts with Esther's enthronement banquet (4).[4] This chapter focuses mainly on Esther's two banquets (6 and 7), which display her mission in courageously and tactfully outmaneuvering the king and the highest officials through her banquet guest list.

At Esther's banquets four main actors play out their assigned roles—Esther, King Xerxes, Mordecai, and Haman—and all experience reversals of power. Mixing both shrewdness within and innocence without, Esther embodies her names of duplicity—

---

[3] For an insightful analysis of the ten banquets in the book of Esther, see Carol M. Bechel, *Esther: Interpretation: A Bible Commentary for Teaching and Preaching* (Louisville, KY: John Knox Press, 2002), 5–6.

[4] Ibid., 5.

Hadassah, righteousness like a myrtle that has both a sweet smell and bitter taste; and Esther, hiddenness.

FIVE RISKS

Esther takes at least five major risks: (1) Concealing her Jewish ethnicity; (2) becoming queen (concealed identity); (3) calling every Jew to a three-day fast (Purim); (4) appearing at the king's court without his summons; and (5) hosting a series of banquets. All five risks taken by Esther, as well as those taken by Mordecai, involve meticulous decision-making by the Jews in the Persian court. According to Greene, "The better you are at dealing with power, the better friend, lover, husband, wife, and person you become."[5] Esther becomes better and better in dealing with the king and his palace people.

Concealed Jewish Ethnicity

Seasoned leaders have a saying about being politically savvy: *Don't volunteer unnecessary information.* In order to hide her Jewishness, Hadassah (righteousness) enters the Persian palace with a Persian name, Esther (hiddenness). Esther conceals her nationality and family background as Mordecai advises (2:10). Hiding one's identity and entering into enemy space would be quite nerve-racking, especially since the Persian court had committed genocide against the Jews and Esther's parents had been killed by the Persian regime.

Becoming Queen

Esther, an orphan who has been raised by her cousin Mordecai, enters into the enemy's palace and succeeds the deposed Queen

---

[5] Greene, *The 48 Laws of Power*, 6.

Vashti (2:17), who is being punished for her revolt against patriarchal demands. Greene offers a countercultural strategy for
dealing with enemies that seems to explain Mordecai's and Esther's
approach to the Persian palace:

> Be wary of friends—they will betray you more quickly, for
> they are easily aroused to envy. They also become spoiled
> and tyrannical. But hire a former enemy and he will be more
> loyal than a friend, because he has more to prove. In fact,
> you have more to fear from friends than from enemies. If
> you have no enemies, find a way to make them.[6]

Indeed, Mordecai and Esther befriend their enemies. Usually
people disengage from their enemies, not engage with them, let
alone marry them. We all have been burned and crushed by our
friends, as Greene explains. I am not advocating making enemies,
but engaging them at the right time could benefit both parties for
a purpose as long as we Asian Pacific Islanders can "place our iron
hand inside a velvet glove."[7] Talk, indeed, is cheap, but actually
engaging the enemy is rare and notable.

"Power requires the ability to play with appearances: to this
end you must learn to wear many masks and keep a bag full of
deceptive tricks."[8] Greene's statement risks misunderstanding
and thus merits explanation. Does the end (the mission) justify
the means? Not necessarily. When Esther takes a bold risk by
entering into the enemy's space with a hidden identity, it shows
the character of her new name, Esther (concealment). In navigating the system it is sometimes necessary to conceal one's identity
until the right time comes. It was her extraordinary beauty that
granted her an entry ticket to King Xerxes's palace as his queen.
However, it was her inner mantra of "if I perish, I perish" that led
Esther to host a series of banquets that spared her people from

---

[6] Ibid., 1.

[7] Robert Greene's quote from Napoléon Bonaparte in *The 48 Laws
of Power* (London: Profile Books LTS, 2000), xviii.

[8] Ibid.

Haman's impending genocide plot. Often the action of solidarity with the "othered" requires courage such as Esther's—through a spirituality of "if I perish, I perish."

Life sometimes presents us with such a risky moment. For example, at one of my first luncheons in a faculty position, the associate provost of color presented a taskforce report on structural diversity. When I entered the room, I quickly noticed that no other taskforce members had shown up. In the middle of his presentation the white-only board members challenged his authority and treated him as an inferior, while placing themselves into the superior position of school ownership. Shocked by the huge disparity between the rhetoric of diversity and the racialized treatment of this Black Latino associate provost, I called out the injustice. The most important thing at that moment was not yielding to the power play waged by the board members. It was my moment of declaring "if I perish, I perish" rather than holding on to my faculty position, which ceased to have meaning and which I subsequently lost. I learned that there is a different kind of power when one relinquishes attachment. Showing the courage to refuse to be threatened by a power play can be quite annoying to the powerful elites.

Purim

Esther, in calling for collective fasting among the Jewish people before she embarks on her mission, sets the tone of her mission and exemplifies courage. Courage involves action despite fear. Without courage, Esther would have not been able to execute the meticulous and savvy plans required for her mission. Rollo May, in *The Courage to Create*, describes courage as follows: "A chief characteristic of courage requires a centeredness within our own being. . . . Therefore, it is the foundation that underlies and gives reality to all other virtues and personal values. Without courage, our love pales into mere dependency."[9] For Queen

---

[9] Rollo May, *The Courage to Create* (New York: W. W. Norton, 1975), 3.

Esther, it was her summoning of a collective three-day fast that centered her inner self within the Persian palace, focused on a divine mission for her people. Such an act revealed her courage and commitment. The required mission and the person to execute it matched seamlessly. The extraordinary personality that imbues the spirituality of "if I perish, I perish" made the "mission impossible" possible.

Many cross-cultural mission endeavors are botched by a mismatch between mission and personnel. In this case Esther's qualities, despite her young age, demonstrate the maturity of a sage, raised and coached by her cousin Mordecai. It is when she called for collective fasting that she becomes a queen with a mission beyond wearing a gown and royal crown. No wonder Jewish people today celebrate Purim to remember how they were spared by Esther's courage. The short attention spans and scattered interests of contemporary people surely need the kind of spiritual anchoring seen in Esther's Purim feasts and her motto of "if I perish, I perish." When one does not cling to life, one is free to execute the mission despite the risks involved: "Whoever tries to keep their life will lose it, and whoever loses their life will preserve it" (Lk 17:33). This selflessness is depicted by Lao Tzu as wu wei: "The reason why heaven and earth are eternal and lasting is because they do not live for themselves; that is the reason they will ever endure."[10] During the Japanese occupation in Korea, a young Korean Methodist student of the early 1900s, Yu Kwan Soon, known as the Korean Joan of Arc, reminds me of a similar spirit of "if I perish, I perish":

> At the age of thirteen, Yu followed the missionary to Seoul, leaving her parents and friends behind. During her school years, Yu was inspired by the biographies of Joan of Arc and Florence Nightingale. Strongly identifying with these two women, naturally Yu was inflamed with a vision of liberating

---

[10] "Wu Wei," an interpretation by Henri Borel, trans. M. E. Reynolds, in *Forgotten Books: Laotzu's Tao and Wu Wei* (New York: Brentano's Publishers, 1919), 16–17.

the motherland as Joan of Arc and sought to have an angelic heart like Florence Nightingale. . . . Within three years of her study in Seoul, the March First Independence Movement began. She could hear the thunder of liberation from the crowds outside her dorm. When she heard that her village was left out of this independence movement, Yu headed down to her village to organize people. Yu demonstrated unusual leadership qualities for such a young age. . . . The night before the scheduled demonstration, she personally climbed the mountain and ignited the fire to signal the gathering the following day at Aunae Market. Yu addressed the crowd, read the declaration, and led a march through town. The Japanese responded with brutal force, killing many people, including Yu's parents and arresting many others. And Yu Kwan Soon was arrested and the flame of the independence movement in Yu Kwan Soon burned even stronger in the prison cell.[11]

Yu Kwan Soon exudes a paradoxical duality of yin and yang: a pacifistic inner surrender to death (yin), and subversive outer social resistance (yang), which Carl Jung refers to as animus, the masculine energy of a female.

It is fascinating that Carl Jung found the answer in Taoism to his question for unity and synchronicity of the opposite types of personality. "The Taoist insistence on a balance between inner and outer, between yin and yang confirmed in Jung's mind that both sides were essential for the development of the self."[12]

Approaching the King without a Summons

Esther's bold action of risking her life by showing up without a summons effectively reverses the king's summoning power that

---

[11] Young Lee Hertig, "Korean Women's Resistance: 'If I Perish, I Perish,'" in *Resistance and Theological Ethics*, ed. Ronald H. Stone and Robert L. Stivers (Lanham, MD: Rowman and Littlefield, 2004), 226–27.

[12] Harold Coward, "Taoism and Jung: Synchronicity and the Self," *Philosophy East and West* 46, no. 4 (October 1996): 477–95.

could end her life. The very act of appearing before her husband was an act of defiance, not submission, which could have gotten Esther killed. Esther prompts King Xerxes to bend his own rules, and he welcomes her. This mission from outside transforms both the Jewish people and the power dynamics of the Persian court. The unlikely reversal of power between the king and queen is quite notable.

Hosting a Series of Banquets

The story of the dispelled Queen Vashti must have been widespread, and Queen Esther, as her successor, would have heard about the infamous and subversive palace women's banquet that deposed Vashti from her queenship. Esther's bold and meticulous contextual actions—in hosting her own series of banquets—earns her enough favor with the king to reverse an impending genocide plot by Haman, the king's top official.

It cannot be overstated how much courage and faith it would have taken for her to enter the enemy's palace while hiding her identity. Esther indeed places her "iron hand inside a velvet glove" and outmaneuvers her opponents. In fact, she masters the art of outmaneuvering. Furthermore, Mordecai set this example of being savvy in exile (not in a survival mode); he is depicted as walking "back and forth near the courtyard of the harem to find out how Esther was and what was happening to her" (2:11). It is likely that Mordecai served as one of the porters at the main entrance to the palace, and in that capacity managed to gain information about her progress. This reveals his shrewd way of living in the midst of persecution in defense of the very existence of the Jews, an approach passed on to his adopted daughter, Esther.

Power brokering is one of the silent but salient issues in both seminaries and churches. According to *Webster's New College Dictionary*, a *power broker* refers to "a person who has power and influence, especially one who operates unofficially or behind the scenes as an intermediary."[13] Institutions are loaded with

---

[13] *Webster's New World College Dictionary,* 5th ed. (Boston: Houghton Mifflin Harcourt, 2014).

unhealthy power dynamics. Often the "all boys" networks prevent women from leadership roles or decision-making. According to Willie James Jennings, "Patriarchy produces a counterfeit vision of God that easily aligns itself with a Christian doctrine of God, kills it, and then replaces it with itself."[14] For this reason many Asian American female pastors still suffer from gender inequality and gender inequity. A female pastor in my mentorship group recently shared about her transition out of ministry service at a vibrant congregation after fourteen years. She no longer had the energy to challenge the obstacles placed before women's ordination. Unemployed while searching for a pastoral position for some time now, she fears the unknown and financial implications of her decision. In contrast, a male pastor friend, during the same year, transitioned out of ten years of ministry at a local congregation and seamlessly found his next leadership position at a multicultural congregation. Promoted to a larger congregation with a larger staff, he does not have to worry about the unknown. The gender disparity is alarming. Most likely, the female pastor will not find another position in an Asian Pacific Islander church. The experience of Asian Pacific Islander female ministers contributes to the rising attrition rate among Asian Pacific Islander pastors at large.

CONTEMPORARY APPLICATION

Upon choosing to exit from an endowed-chair position in a theological institution in 2002, I now see myself as a theological-missional broker and thus resonate deeply with both Vashti and Esther. Like Vashti, I bucked the system when it sapped my life-giving energy. I find Vashti's choice to be in solidarity with the palace women—the king's objects for his own pleasure and

---

[14] Willie James Jennings, "A Christian Vision of Belonging: Gender Identity in the Church," in *Society of Asian North American Christian Studies 2014–2015 Journal* (Los Angeles, CA: Innovative Space for Asian American Christianity, 2015), 32.

design—life giving and life risking. Seemingly, it would have been in her self-interest, rather than a self-sacrifice, to choose to be in solidarity with the palace women for their human dignity, even momentarily. Jesus's paradoxical truth sheds light on this issue: "For whoever wants to save their life will lose it, but whoever loses their life for me and for the gospel will save it" (Mk 8:35). There are times in life when one is called to make courageous and risky decisions simply to keep souls intact. Vashti's disobedience to the king's demand and her exemplary action of organizing a women's banquet as an alternative to the king's created an authentic and powerful initiative that led to an unintended consequence: a huge threat to the patriarchy. In response to Vashti's actions, King Xerxes becomes powerless, desperately consulting all kinds of experts, including astrologists.

In Queen Esther, I find a gentle savviness that utilizes the system to execute the mission of sparing her people from a planned genocide. Working the system for others, rather than for oneself, is rare in today's culture of "selfies" and narcissism. In Esther's story I see what I call EGG (Ethnicity, Gender, Generation) working in seamless synchronicity, which often propagates more conflict, even leading to wars as beliefs collide.

It is noble for the Persian King Xerxes to act counter-culturally when he chooses solidarity with the queen's ethnicity. It is likewise noble for a young Jewish queen to navigate the mission of saving her people from a death plot by soliciting the king's favor and arranging alternative plans right under his nose through a series of banquets. It is also noble to see a father figure, Mordecai, working with Esther through mutual respect and reciprocity in carrying out a seemingly impossible mission. These examples are much needed today when power abuse is on raw display and threatens law and order as well as democracy and integrity. Ethnicity is often a discrediting factor in public policies and procedures. In addition to women mentors, it is important for women leaders to have male mentors like Mordecai when dealing with patriarchal power structures. Across gender and generation, Mordecai and Esther together meticulously execute their bold and risky mission of "if I perish, I perish" as they show what it takes to be power brokers with "velvet gloves" when working within the parameters of Xerxes's palace.

The celebration of Purim, even today, retells the stories of God's provision for the Jews in exile through their entrance into the Persian palace. The implications for the Diaspora in the book of Esther speak to issues of violence and tension that intensify and deepen in the present. The stories of Esther and Mordecai could also serve as an intergenerational and gender bridge today, which is rare, but much needed for a mission bigger than each generation. Language barriers in immigrant communities disconnect generations, which causes a scarcity of intergenerational bridges. Collaboration between male and female leaders in faith communities also poses a challenge due to the dominance of complementarian rather than egalitarian gender roles. Mordecai and Esther provide a contrast to this norm through their egalitarian collaboration.

Male and female faith leaders must work compassionately and meticulously in God's beloved world, which is plagued by inequalities and exclusionary systems of power. Daring to say no to abusive power and to organize people on the margins threatens the systems in place. Once we wean ourselves off our addiction to self-interest and self-promotion, then transformation may be of the people, by the people, and for the people, thus restoring the image of God for both male and female, insiders and outsiders, all for the greater mission of God. Indeed, throughout the Bible, God utilizes many outsiders to teach insiders.

In the story of Esther, Jews in exile transform the Persian king and influence his decision-making. In the dynamic encounter of Jews and Gentiles, both need paradigm shifts as they engage each other. In fact, King Xerxes ends up bending his policy for Esther after she risks her life by entering into the king's palace. Both are transformed by the encounter of the "other" through intense negotiating and navigating.

Despite several waves of feminism and more recent discourses on postcolonial and eco-feminism in academia, male dominance of pulpits on Sunday persists, often with the exception of white women clergy. On the rare occasions that women clergy are hired, they are paid less than their male counterparts. This results in the silencing of women's voices despite their numerical majority in the church. Church women who internalize patriarchal culture gladly remain pew sitters, while many who desire gender equity exit the church due to perceived irrelevance; this is especially true of younger women and men. This will continue to have an effect on the sociopolitical fabric of the United States.

Toward a fuller expression of the body of Christ, addressing the problem of male-gendered pulpits and implementing transformation require collaboration of both male clergy and female pastors. Will complementarian megachurches yield their power to accommodate gender equality and gender equity as King Xerxes did?

To tackle contemporary gender disparity in the church, ISAAC (Innovative Space for Asian American Christianity) submitted a grant proposal titled "Imagining a More Equal Pulpit" (in Asian Pacific Islander and Latinx congregations) to the Louisville Institute in March 2017, and a Collaborative Inquiry team has been working to document the best practices of gender-inclusive pulpits. This led to a Gender Summit in 2018, in which influencers and decision-makers gathered to listen to the stories from women leaders and strategized to bring about changes.

ISAAC is planning a plenary inspired by Esther's banquet with key players who envision more equal pulpits in Asian Pacific Islander and Latinx congregations in Southern California and beyond. The invitees include both male and female biblical scholars and pastors from both communities, since gender-inclusive pulpits cannot be created without male allies. I imagine a series of "Esther's banquets" that require both shrewdness within (yang) and innocence without (yin) in collaboration with allies, as Mordecai was for Esther. Navigating changes in the pulpits requires seasoned politics and the collaboration of both male and female faith leaders, just as we saw in the time of Esther.

Chapter 7

The Magi and Matthew's Approach to the Religions

Paul Hertig

Migrants who arrive in a new land are often able to interpret the signs of the times and decipher their new context more clearly and objectively than insiders who are myopically entrenched in their own layers of immediate reality. Furthermore, migrants whose religion intersects with the religion of the new context inform the religion in the new context and also become informed by that religious context. The dynamic is interactive and transformative. In the study at hand, prophecy in the migrants' religion intersects with prophecy in the new context. Each informs the other, and the interchange influences both the visiting migrants and the host country. In contemporary global reality, migrants initiate a range of changes in the host country, from fear, to selective accommodation, to assimilation. Migration in Los Angeles, for instance, now majority Latinx, has changed the cultural and religious landscape there. Responses to the influx of Latinx immigrants range from fear to support, from "they are stealing our jobs and raising our crime rate" to "this land was stolen from them and now they are taking it back."

The initial response to the Magi, who traversed "from the east" into Jerusalem, was one of fear and anguish. The Magi humbly asked, based on their reading of the signs of the times, "Where is the one who has been born king of the Jews? We saw his star when it rose and have come to worship him." The immediate response: "When King Herod heard this he was disturbed, and all Jerusalem with him" (Mt 2:1–3). Because culture, politics, and religion intertwine, the political and religious leaders of the day were disturbed about the impact that the migrants might have on society. Specifically, culture, politics, and religion, in the Jerusalem context, exhibited heightened expectation for a new messianic era.

STARS AND MESSIANIC EXPECTATION

Due to widespread belief in astrology in ancient days, the stars were believed to foretell the future, and the star under which one was born determined one's destiny. Since stars represent the order of the universe, the sudden appearance of a brilliant star meant that God was interrupting the natural order to reveal something extraordinary.[1] In the era of Jesus, in particular, whether presaged by a star or other phenomena, there was widespread expectation of the coming of a unique king. A Jewish sect, the Qumran community, set up camp in the desert in anticipation of the coming of the Messiah, as indicated in the Dead Sea Scrolls: "His wisdom will reach all the peoples, and he will know the secrets of all the living. And all their designs against him will come to nothing and his rule over all the living will be great" (Book of Noah, Fragment 4Q534).

The Magi's specific observation of "his star," the one born king of the Jews at its rising (Mt 2:2), signifies a belief that each child is born under a certain pattern of stars and that each child has "his/her star."[2] The scriptures here seem to point to a general

---

[1] Jean Danielou, *The Infancy Narratives*, trans. Rosemary Sheed (New York: Herder and Herder, 1968), 76; William Barclay, *Good Tidings of Great Joy: The Birth of Jesus the Messiah* (Louisville, KY: Westminster John Knox Press, 1999), 89–90.

[2] Danielou, *The Infancy Narratives.*, 76.

revelation given to those outside the Jewish faith. "The testimony of Scriptures (2:5) is supported by the testimony of nature."[3] Matthew depicts an intimate relationship between God and nature (Mt 5:45; 10:29; 27:45–53). This interrelationship opens up an interreligious dynamic, as we see throughout the second chapter in Matthew.

The star that shines brightly in the night to reveal the king of the Jews, whom the Magi seek, is founded on themes in Isaiah 60, specifically the following verses that stress light, brightness, dawn, the nations, gold and incense, and the worship of the Lord (italicized in the three following categories):

> "Arise, shine, for your *light* has come . . .
>> and the glory of the LORD rises upon you. (v. 1)
> [1] Nations will come to your *light*,
>> and kings to the *brightness* of your *dawn*. (v. 3)
>> . . .
>> To you the riches of the *nations* will come. (v. 5)
>> . . .
> [2] bearing *gold* and *incense*
> and [3] proclaiming the *praise of the LORD*." (v. 6)

These verses provide the backdrop for the universal and biblical context of the Magi, who are Gentiles entering the Holy Land in holy procession, seeking the sacred birth of a worldwide king.

THE ORIGINS OF THE MAGI: ZOROASTRIANISM

The Magi are introduced with the term *behold*, a word which "arouses attention" and indicates that they are "extraordinary visitors."[4] Coming "from the east" (Mt 2:1) could refer to regions

---

[3] W. D. Davies and Dale C. Allison, *Matthew 1–7*, vol. 1, International Critical Commentary (New York: A and C Black, 2004), 233.

[4] Ibid., 227; see ASV and KJV for "behold."

in Arabia, Babylon, or Persia. While the debate among these three is beyond the scope of this chapter, we home in on the most likely origin of the term *magi,* that of the Medes of the Persian Empire (modern-day Iran). Early "Syriac traditions give the Magi Persian names. Christian art in the second-century Roman catacombs dresses them in Persian garments; a majority of early church fathers interpret them as Persian."[5] Furthermore, invading Persians in 614 CE spared the destruction of the Church of the Nativity due to wise men depicted in Persian headdress in a mosaic above the entrance.[6]

Historically associated with the ancient Median priests, diviners, and religious mediators of pre-Achaemenid Persia (prior to 550 BCE), the expression *magi* also carries with it the extensive history of Zoroastrian religious practice that depicts those who specialize in ritual ceremonies including sacrifices, chants, invocations, and divination.[7] It is crucial to note that centuries prior to the writing of Matthew's Gospel, beginning in the fourth century BCE, classical authors referred to Zoroaster as a magus and his followers as magi.[8]

Thus, the term *magi* referred to (1) Zoroastrian priests; and (2) participants in a private ritual in an effort to affect history in the present or future. Syriac and Arabic sources refer to such a person as a "magian," "head of the magians," "chief of the sect," "magian prophet," or "diviner." Zoroaster, in the classics of Greece and Rome, "was the arch-representative of the Magi . . . regarded as a great sage and as a prophet whose name was synonymous with Persian wisdom, or the founder of the Magian priesthood who are sometimes said to be his pupils and followers." The Magi "were the reputed masters of learning in ancient times, and Zoroaster

---

[5] Paul L. Maier, *First Christmas: The True and Unfamiliar Story in Words and Pictures* (New York: Harper and Row, 1971), 67.

[6] Ibid.

[7] Roy Kotansky, "The Star of the Magi: Lore and Science in Ancient Zoroastrianism, the Greek Magical Papyra and St. Matthew's Gospel," *Annali di Storia dell' Esegesi* 24, no. 2 (2007): 392.

[8] Davies and Allison, *Matthew 1–7,* 227–28.

stood for this learning in antiquity."[9] At their finest, magi were depicted as moral and holy sages who sought truth.

These connotations began long before the term *magi* became derogatorily correlated with fortunetellers, sorcerers, magicians, and charlatans who eventually turned up in various magical writings, including the Greek Magical Papyri.[10] The negative or positive use of the term *magi* was historically determined by its social, cultural, and religious context. The positive and popular interpretation that Matthew's Magi were Zoroastrian priests from the Median religious order stems from the fact that Matthew's Magi have none of the negative trappings of the term, which will be explained later. As Ray Kotansky notes, "In the Gospel, they are figures of great respect."[11] The Iranian prophet Zoroaster had earlier received unparalleled and widespread admiration in the Greco-Roman context of approximately 1000 BCE (though this date may be up to two hundred years earlier).[12]

In the writings of Herodotus, magi perform offerings, sacrifices, and hymns. They interpret signs and dreams and even serve in the court as officials with administrative and legal responsibility. This indicates their distinguished status.

Ahura Mazda and the Bright Star

Greco-Roman literature in the New Testament era indicates attentiveness to the Zoroastrian focus on one particular star that appears in rituals documented in the Greek Magical Papyri. This star, one of the brightest, reigns over the constellation of the Great Dog, Sirius, established as the great guardian in the night sky as declared in a Zoroastrian hymn: "the bright glorious star

---

[9] A. V. Williams Jackson, *Zoroaster: The Prophet of Ancient Iran* (New York: Columbia University Press, 1938), 6, 7.

[10] Kotansky, "The Star of the Magi," 392. The Greek Magical Papyri from Greco-Roman Egypt date from the second century BCE to the fifth century CE.

[11] Ibid., 393.

[12] Ibid.

Tistrya, whom Ahura Mazda established as a lord and overseer of all stars."[13] The same hymn states, "We sacrifice unto Tistrya, the bright glorious star, who stunts the growth of all, who washes away all things of fear . . . and brings health to all creations."[14] This indicates an important contextual backdrop of the star that the Magi followed to Bethlehem. Ahura Mazda, who oversees the stars, is central to Zoroastrian religion and

> sits at the apex among the celestial beings. Beyond him, apart from him, and without him, nothing exists. He is the Supreme Being through whom everything exists. He is brighter than the brightest of creation, higher than the highest heavens, older than the oldest universe. . . . He is changeless. He is the same now and forever. . . . He is the Lord of all.[15]

The "brighter than the brightest" is nuanced in the sun and stars. Ahura Mazda, the Supreme Being, comes from these roots: *Ahura* means "lord" and *Mazda* means "wisdom"—literally, "the Lord Wisdom," or "the Wise Lord."[16]

The original apocalyptic texts state, "Ahura Mazda created many good creatures . . . in order that they shall make the world wonderful, . . . in order that the dead shall rise up, that the Living One, the Indestructible, shall come, the world be made wonderful at his wish."[17] Thus Ahura Mazda represents supreme lordship *and* resurrection, and also, we now see, divine truth: "From the very mouth of Mazda the prophet yearns to know the divine truth, in order that he and his adherents may convert all living

---

[13] Ibid., 394; F. Max Muller, *The Zend Avesta* (Abingdon, UK: Routledge, 2013), 105.

[14] Muller, *The Zend Avesta*, 105.

[15] Maneckji Nusservanji Dhalla, *Zoroastrian Theology* (New York: AMS Press, 1972), 19–20.

[16] Ibid., 19; F. M. Kotwal and J. W. Boyd, *A Guide to the Zoroastrian Religion* (Chico, CA: Scholars Press, 1982), 4.

[17] Mary Boyce, ed. and trans., *Textual Sources for the Study of Zoroastrianism* (Totowa, NJ: Barnes and Noble, 1984), 90.

men to the excellent faith." In addition, the Zoroastrian saint's mission aspires for justice, "for the advancement of the world is to live in society and minister to the wants and grievances of the less fortunate of mankind."[18]

It is no wonder that the Magi, rooted in Zoroastrian religion, would marvel at the idea of a divine savior, namely Jesus, who exhibited parallel attributes to Ahura Mazda, and upon whom shone the bright star, parallel to Ahura Mazda's bright and glorious star, Tistrya. Raymond E. Brown observes that the church fathers, beginning with Clement of Alexandria, believed that Zoroaster "was a prophet who predicted the coming of the Messiah," which points to a Persian background for Matthew's Magi.[19]

The Virgin Birth

The Zoroastrians believed in the Saoshyant (savior or he who will bring good fortune).[20] The Saoshyant refers to one who establishes a religious kingdom of righteousness on earth. Gradually the concept of Saoshyant became an end-of-the-world expectation, when the powers of evil would finally be defeated. The victorious Saoshyant "will make the world most excellent, unageing, undecaying, neither passing away nor falling into corruption; for ever shall it live and for ever prosper."[21]

The parallels with the Jewish expectation of a Messiah are rich, yet even more striking are parallels to the Matthean virgin birth. An ancient account states that the light and power of Zoroaster's own seed was preserved at the bottom of a sacred lake and that it

---

[18] Dhalla, *Zoroastrian Theology*, 13, 15.

[19] Raymond E. Brown, *Birth of the Messiah* (New York: Image, 1979), 168.

[20] R. C. Zaehner, "Zoroastrianism," in *Encyclopedia of the World's Religions*, ed. R. C. Zaehner, 200–214 (New York: Barnes and Noble Books, 1997), 208.

[21] Ibid., translated from *Yasht* 19:89–90. It is likely that this eschatological nuance arose during the Achaemenian period and became further developed in later literature.

would miraculously impregnate a virgin who would bathe there at the appointed time and whose offspring would become the savior.[22] The ancient text states that "it will be thus: a virgin will go to Lake Kayansih to bathe; and the Glory (of Zardusht) will enter her body, and she will become with child."[23]

Once the Savior appears, bodies are raised from the dead. The long-term expectation of a divine savior from Zoroaster's lineage weighed heavily upon the shoulders of a pre-Christian, first-century-BCE populace, and intermingled with prophecies within Judaism and early Christianity, laying behind the historical events of Matthew's Magi. Since there were similarities and not significant differences between Judaism and Zoroastrianism, the Magi may have believed that the Saoshyant (savior) had been born, and this may have set them on their journey to discover the king of the Jews. How they may have correlated the two events— their virgin birth account and the Jewish virgin birth—would be interesting to explore.[24]

THE MAGI ARE GENTILES

While not every scholar believes that the Magi were Gentiles,[25] I find the case for Gentiles is convincing. I build my chapter around this argument, which leads down the road to an important connection between the Magi and Zoroastrianism, one that parallels the Magi and Balaam. Here are the major indicators that the Magi were Gentiles:

---

[22] Brown, *Birth of the Messiah*, 169; Kotansky, "The Star of the Magi," 398.

[23] Boyce, *Textual Sources for the Study of Zoroastrianism*, 91.

[24] Zaehner, "Zoroastrianism," 208. Richard R. Racy, *Nativity: The Christmas Story, Which You Have Never Heard Before* (Bloomington, IN: Author House, 2007), 142. Although a much later reference, this link is made in approximately the sixth century in the apocryphal writing *Arabic Gospel of the Infancy*, 7:1: "Some magi came to Jerusalem to the prediction of the Zoroaster" (see Brown, *Birth of the Messiah*, 168).

[25] David C. Sim, "The Magi: Gentiles or Jews?" *HTS Teologiese Studies/ Theological Studies* 55 (1999): 980–1000.

1. When the Magi enter Jerusalem, they ask for the whereabouts of the "king of the Jews." This phrase is found only on the lips of Gentiles in all four Gospels and in the New Testament as a whole, and is common in non-Christian sources. The Jews, on the other hand, use the phrase, "king of Israel" (for example, Mt 27:42).[26]

2. The Magi are wise men but appear to be not well acquainted with Jewish scriptures; they have to ask where the Messiah will be born (2:2–6). They also appear to be unacquainted with the political situation, because they openly talk to Herod about this and, without intention, encroach upon his authority.

3. The Magi seek Jesus through natural revelation—a star—representing the best of Gentile wisdom and religious perception. Magi and astrologers were renowned in the Greco-Roman context as "able to recognize the signs of the times to foretell events of world importance, including the rise of kings." Cicero alleges that Persian Magi "prophesied on the night of Alexander's birth that one newly born would threaten all of Asia."[27]

Ancient astrologers claimed that the conjunction of certain constellations announced the birth of a king and that a comet indicated a change of emperor, and popular belief suggested that "stars rose with people, bright for the rich, small for the poor, dim for those worn out."[28] In Commagene, near the northeast border of Syria, possibly where the Gospel of Matthew was written, astrology thrived. There, a horoscope was unearthed of the Roman client-king Antiochus I (69–31 BCE), who reigned just prior to the birth of Jesus. "The principle of astrology is to establish a horoscope based on the sign of the zodiac that is rising in the eastern horizon when a person is born."[29] The Magi in Matthew play this particular role typical of the Greco-Roman world, not

---

[26] Davies and Allison, *Matthew 1–7*, 233.

[27] Ibid., 230.

[28] Ibid., 233.

[29] Brown, *Birth of the Messiah*, 173.

to deny negative depictions of Magi in historical accounts. These
Magi "are the mysterious wise foreigners who, having mastered"
secret wisdom to discern a new king, glorify Jesus.[30] Zoroastrianism epitomizes the many examples of wisdom traditions that
come from contexts inside and outside of Judaism, and implicitly
or explicitly lay the foundation for future revelation.[31] Thomas
Aquinas, in his *Summa Theologiae*, states perceptively: "The
Magi are the 'first-fruits of the Gentiles' that believed in Christ;
because their faith was a [sign] of the faith and devotion of the
nations who were to come to Christ from afar. And therefore . . .
we must believe that the Magi, inspired by the Holy Ghost, did
wisely in paying homage to Christ."[32]

Wisdom Enters Judaism from Outside and Challenges Authority

The Magi do not fit the negative depictions given in early
Christian sources (for example, Ignatius, or Acts 8:9–11) or by
Pharaoh's sorcerers (Ex 7:10–12), but they do fit positive depictions (such as those by Philo of Alexandria).[33] For example: (1)
the Magi do not oppose Jesus but offer gifts and worship with
great rejoicing; (2) the Magi refuse to conspire with Herod and
thus protect the baby Jesus from harm; (3) they are *not* depicted
as "Magi from Egypt," which would provide negative parallelism

---

[30] Davies and Allison, *Matthew 1–7*, 230.

[31] Karen Armstrong, *The Great Transformation: The Beginning of Our
Religious Traditions* (New York: Alfred A. Knopf, 2006), 12–14.

[32] Thomas Aquinas, *Summa Theologiae*, III. Q. 36, Art. 8, answer.

[33] "And in the land of the barbarians, in which the same men are
authorities both as to words and actions, very numerous companies of
virtuous and honorable men are celebrated. Among the Persians there
is the body of the Magi, who, investigating the works of nature for the
purpose of becoming acquainted with the truth, do at their leisure become
initiated themselves and initiate others in the divine virtues by very clear
explanations" (Philo, *The Works of Philo*, "Every Good Man Is Free,"
XI [74]).

with Pharaoh's Magi; and (4) when the Magi informed King Herod that they had come to worship the king of the Jews, Herod was disturbed, and all Jerusalem with him (Mt 2:3). A sharp contrast is drawn between the disturbed Herod and Jewish leadership, and the worshipful Magi. The Magi pursued "the king of the Jews," but, ironically, this was also Herod's title, and he took this as a direct challenge to his own position of authority.

The ideals of a messianic king in Judaism, as expressed by Isaiah the prophet, were not unlike what Roman poets articulated regarding the age of Augustus. The Roman emperor from 27 BCE to 14 CE, Augustus was acclaimed as both divine *and* savior of the world. Augustus also prided himself for ushering in a reign of peace.[34] "Peace in terms of an end to warfare, harmony in nature, and justice among peoples were standard themes. Could it be that the astute Herod sought to tap into those Jewish hopes in order to legitimate his espousal of Augustan aspirations for more personal ends?"[35] In fact, Herod took advantage of Jewish hopes for a messiah by erecting a new temple in which it would please Yahweh to dwell (Qumran *Temple Scroll*: 11QTemple 51).[36] These historical factors indicate why all of Jerusalem was disturbed along with Herod, assuming they had bought into the Herodian concept of the messiah, and also why Herod pretended to buy into the Jewish concept of the messiah for his own ends by cunningly asking the Magi to tell him the whereabouts of the birth of the king of the Jews so that he might worship him (2:8).

This contrast represents the first kernel of Matthew's extensive theme contrasting the unbelief of Jewish leadership with the astounding belief of Gentiles. The Magi account is an early indicator of the universality of the mission of Jesus. Jesus is not just king of the Jews but king of the entire world, which becomes crystal clear at the culmination of the Gospel when Jesus sends the

---

[34] Seán Freyne, *The Jesus Movement and Its Expansion: Meaning and Mission* (Grand Rapids, MI: Eerdmans, 2014), 53, 163; Barclay, *Good Tidings of Great Joy*, 90.

[35] Freyne, *The Jesus Movement and Its Expansion*, 56.

[36] Ibid.

disciples to all nations (28:16–20). Furthermore, the procession of Gentiles coming to worship Jesus prefigures the flowing in of Gentiles into Matthew's own community. This Matthean Gentile theme that begins with the procession of the Magi is rooted in Balaam, where "magic" and "magi" intersect.

The Balaam Connection

Balaam, a Gentile, was called a magus by the Jewish writer Philo. Balaam practiced his arts with both good and evil intent.[37] Matthew depended on the principal narrative of Balaam in the book of Numbers (22—24), which promotes Balaam's good side. In the passage, Balaam came from the east, accompanied by two servants—a party of three—and interrupted King Balak's antagonistic plans to put a curse on Israel (Num 23:27) by declaring the future greatness of Israel and the ascent of a royal king (Num 24:1–9).

Note the parallels between Balaam and the Magi: (1) the Magi come from the east; (2) they foil the plans of the King (Herod), who wanted to use the Magi to abolish his enemy; and (3) the Magi instead honored his enemy. The story of Balaam provides the backdrop of Matthew's account of the Magi.[38] With that backdrop we now explore excerpts from Balaam's prophecy in Numbers:

> And when Balaam saw that it pleased God to bless Israel, he did not go according to his custom to meet the omens, but turned his face toward the wilderness. And Balaam lifted up his eyes, and sees Israel encamped by their tribes; and the Spirit of God came upon him. And he took up his parable and said, Balaam son of Beor says, the man who sees truly

---

[37] Balaam's good side: rather than cursing Israel as Balak urged, Balaam blessed Israel. His evil side: the Bible imputed Balaam when men of Israel were seduced into idolatry through Moabite women. But it is likely that the negative biblical accounts of Revelation 2:14, Jude 11, and 2 Peter 2:15, 16 were penned after the completion of Matthew's Gospel.

[38] Brown, *Birth of the Messiah*, 89.

says, he says who hears the oracle of the Mighty One, who saw a vision of God in sleep; his eyes were opened: How goodly *are* thy habitations, Jacob, and thy tents, Israel! as shady groves, and as gardens by a river, and as tents which God pitched, and as cedars by the waters. **There shall come a man out of his seed, and he shall rule over many nations; and the kingdom of God shall be exalted, and his kingdom shall be increased. . . .**

I will point to him, but not now; I bless him, but he draws not near: **a star shall rise out of Jacob,** a man shall spring out of Israel; and shall crush the princes of Moab, and shall spoil all the sons of Seth. (Num 24:1–7, 17, LXX)[39]

The New International Version and other translations, derived from the Hebrew, speak of Balaam falling prostrate in Numbers 24:4: "the prophecy of one who hears the words of God, who sees a vision from the Almighty, who falls prostrate, and whose eyes are opened." This is also an important connecting point to the Magi in Matthew, who fall prostrate at the sight of the baby Jesus (Mt 2:11).

Balaam's prophecy about a star (Num 24:17) was applied to the Messiah by the Qumran community, which interpreted "a star will come forth/rise out of Jacob," as the anticipated Levitical Messiah (CD 7:18–26).[40] Qumran is specifically quoting Numbers 24:17. Those who do not believe that Matthew was mindful of Numbers 24:17 point out that the gospel writer does not cite the verse. However, the absence of the verse is explained by the fact that all four of the formula quotations in Matthew 2 are geographically based, each including a specific region—Bethlehem, Egypt, Ramah, and Nazareth—but Numbers 24:17 does not contain such a geographical reference to suit Matthew's purpose.[41]

---

[39] This quotation is from the Brenton Septuagint (LXX) translation. I have bolded the messianic references.

[40] Davies and Allison, *Matthew 1–7*, 234. The Qumran's reference to Numbers 24:17 is also found in 4QTestimonia and 1QM 11:6.

[41] Davies and Allison, *Matthew 1–7*, 235.

The magus Balaam and Matthew's Magi are parallel in "title, origin, and role"; furthermore, we have the prediction of a rising star that symbolizes the Messiah.[42] The Gentile Magi are privileged to follow this light, and in the Hebrew scriptures Yahweh "revealed His salvific intent to Gentiles. The presence of Gentile worshipers in Matthew's community was not the result of a failure in God's plan for Israel; it was the continuity and fulfillment of a plan of salvation for those from afar to be accomplished through the Messiah and Israel."[43] Thus wisdom tradition that comes from nations beyond Israel plays a critical role in validation of and participation in God's plan. A helpful backdrop to Matthew's positive portrayal of the Magi is this wisdom tradition explained in the scriptures: "Solomon's wisdom was greater than the *wisdom of all the people of the East*, and greater than all the wisdom of Egypt" (1 Kgs 4:30, italics added). The East represents an ambiance for enlightened wisdom. Matthew illuminates the mystique of the East through the only words spoken by the Magi: "Where is the one who has been born king of the Jews? We saw his star when it rose and have come to worship him" (2:2). The Magi's "general silence enhances the aura of mystery about them."[44] People who speak few words are typically deemed wise (Prov 17:27); those who chatter are depicted as fools (Mt 6:7).

Since the Magi may not be well versed in Jewish scriptures, they depend on the priests and scribes to locate where the Messiah will be born. Initially, they elicit knowledge from the Jews; afterward, this norm of Jews enlightening Gentiles is reversed, and the Gentiles act wisely while the particular Jewish leaders do not (the Magi even received a revelatory dream in 2:12). While the Jewish leaders normally excel in knowledge, in this case they do not utilize their knowledge for good purposes; instead the Gentiles do, averting Herod's ploy to kill Jesus.[45] This remarkable portrayal of wisdom tradition demonstrates that knowledge must

---

[42] Brown, *Birth of the Messiah*, 195.

[43] Ibid., 196.

[44] Davies and Allison, *Matthew 1–7*, 232.

[45] Ibid., 239.

be applied. Jesus later states that "wisdom is proved right by her deeds" (Mt 11:19), captured nicely by the J. B. Phillips translation: "wisdom stands or falls by her own actions."[46]

In fact, Matthew's theological agenda fits well with the Balaam background, depicting the positive role of outsiders who migrate from other religious contexts and enter into God's missional agenda. Just as Balaam, the Gentile magus, receives an authentic prophetic revelation from the God of Israel, so the Magi in Matthew receive divine revelation from God through nature that is confirmed in Jewish scripture (2:2, 5). W. D. Davies and Dale C. Allison conclude that Matthew likely considered the Magi to be successors of Balaam, and they were the first witnesses of the fulfillment of the ancient oracle "a star shall rise from Jacob" (Num 24:17, LXX).[47]

What makes the connection most interesting is that Balaam was not a Jew but a Gentile, a wise man, paralleling the Magi. Tradition sometimes identifies Balaam with Zoroaster. Origen felt that the Magi knew Balaam's prophecy, and that when they saw the star rise, they recognized it as a prophetic fulfillment. This elicits an interreligious issue in which one religion's prophecy intersects with another and both are illuminated. Such religious cross-pollination could have occurred, for example, when the Jews were exiled into captivity in Babylon (ca. 597–581 BCE).

Commentators typically see the unidentified and mysterious Magi as "representatives of the best wisdom of the Gentile world, its spiritual elite," and furthermore, "while the Jewish leaders reject their Messiah, the Gentiles from outside the land of Israel are anxious to greet them."[48] Matthew has utilized the nuance of the word *magi* to refer to authentic wisdom that is true and transcends religious barriers.

Zoroastrianism shared several key fundamental beliefs with Judaism. As already shown, both were monotheistic, believed in

---

[46] J. B. Phillips, *The New Testament in Modern English*, rev. ed. (New York: Touchstone, 1995).

[47] Davies and Allison, *Matthew 1–7*, 231.

[48] Ibid., 228.

angels and demons, a devil, judgment and reward, and—like some Jews—resurrection. Though there are differences, "the similarities are so pronounced that secular scholars have concluded that Zoroastrianism was the originating monotheism that generated the religion of Israel and later Islam."[49]

THE UNIVERSAL SCOPE OF MATTHEW AND INTERRELIGIOUS IMPLICATIONS

The Magi account reflects Matthew's own context of the conversion of Gentiles from other religions and persecution from Jewish leadership and Roman political rule. Since it does not make sense for Gentile Magi to come from afar to pay homage to a newborn Jewish messiah figure, this narrative signals a deliberate Matthean agenda of contrasting the unbelief of Jewish leadership with the conversion of Gentiles. The guardians of the Jewish religion's rejection and the Gentile acceptance of Jesus fit the mysterious plan of God from the beginning.[50] It is important to clarify that "all Jerusalem" in Matthew 2:3 represents the center of Jewish leadership, which includes a system of corrupt political leaders. The term *Jerusalem* here does not represent the Jewish people as a whole. Joseph, Mary, and Jesus were Jews, and so were Jesus's twelve disciples, as well as many of the large crowds that followed Jesus. Therefore, *Jerusalem* does not represent the entire Jewish community.

It is crucial to note that compared to the critical role of Jerusalem as the center of God's activity in history, Bethlehem and Nazareth are "insignificant hamlets."[51] But these hamlets host Jesus, which leads to a very important contrast:

Herod, the Pharisees, the scribes, the chief priests, Pilate, Jerusalem—all are associated with power, all oppose Jesus,

---

[49] Racy, *Nativity*, 141.
[50] Danielou, *The Infancy Narratives*, 94–95.
[51] Davies and Allison, *Matthew 1–7*, 238, 239.

and all are rebuked by Matthew. In contrast, Bethlehem and Nazareth, the persecuted parents of Jesus, the twelve disciples—all are lowly, all receive Jesus, and all are exalted by Matthew. In our judgment, scholars in the past have tended to overplay the Gentile/Jew contrast in Matthew and ignore altogether the powerful/powerless contrast. The result has sometimes been the unjustified reading of anti-Judaism into the First Gospel.[52]

Not only is there a reversal of the providence of the powerful and powerless in the Magi account, but even more specifically, there is a reversal of the roles of Gentile and Jew. The migrants outside of Judaism demonstrate wisdom and discernment; the leaders inside demonstrate imprudence and compromise with power. Matthew emphasizes that authentic power arises from wisdom, not from mere knowledge. Wisdom involves sound ethical judgment that is put into action; knowledge involves understanding at the cognitive level. This is the value of the wisdom tradition, whether it comes from the inside or outside the religious center.

The joy of the Magi contrasts with the troubled response of Herod and all Jerusalem. Thus, in the words of Philo, "joy and pleasure do not have intrinsic values, but are by-products of virtue and characterize the sage."[53] Philo believed that joy, an attribute of God, can be transferred to the wise alone. Only the wise one, or sage, is "truly capable of experiencing joy."[54] Thus, only the virtuous one has lasting joy, because wisdom fashions joy, and therefore the Magi are the heroes in the story. Even Herod reiterates their intentions regarding Jesus, stating, "That I too may go and worship him" (Mt 2:8). The only way for Herod to accomplish his goal is to deceive the Magi, thus the text clears the Magi from collusion. They are truly wise men.

---

[52] Ibid., 239.

[53] Marian Hillar, *From Logos to Trinity: The Evolution of Religious Beliefs from Pythagoras to Tertullian* (Cambridge, UK: Cambridge University Press, 2012), 48.

[54] Davies and Allison, *Matthew 1–7*, 247.

Furthermore, the Magi represent seeds planted early in the Gospel that anticipate Jesus's interaction with those of other religions, which lead up to the final mission mandate that crosses both cultural and religious boundaries (28:19–20). The centurion and the Canaanite woman who journey to Jesus from outside the Jewish faith are congratulated by Jesus for their faith and represent additional seeds that lead to the final mission mandate. Amazed by the faith of the centurion, Jesus declares that "many will come from the east and the west, and will take their places at the feast with Abraham, Isaac, and Jacob in the kingdom of heaven" (8:11). Gentile migration from around the world is a kingdom anticipation anchored in the story of the Magi.

Also in the same vein as the Magi, the Canaanite woman kneels down before Jesus and declares him as Lord (15:25), even though Jesus has just acknowledged to her that he was "sent only to the lost sheep of Israel" (15:24). Following her profession of faith, Jesus subsequently congratulates her for her faith and heals her daughter (15:28).

The Magi are foundational for Matthew's theology of the religions. Migrating from afar, with surprising wisdom and discernment, they inform those at the religious and political epicenter of the light of Jesus that shines upon the world. Through natural revelation and age-old wisdom the Magi provide a challenge to contemporary Christians who turn a blind eye to the glimmers of light that shine in surprising places.

Matthew's Gospel begins with one surprising story after another. A humble peasant woman gives birth to Jesus, and religious outsiders are the first to give witness to Jesus and to bow down and worship him. This beginning provides a window into Matthew's theology of the religions, and provides relevance for how we might respond to surprises in a context of religious pluralism today. The contrast Matthew sets up is that although particular Jewish leaders cannot acknowledge God's presence among them, the Magi, who come from afar, not only acknowledge but also worship Jesus. The Gospel informs us not to be surprised by who does and who does not acknowledge Jesus, but to rejoice with those from other religions who have the propensity to recognize him.

CONTEMPORARY APPLICATION

A vivid example of this in the intersection of religions was described to me by Christians in Southeast Asia:

> *A man faithfully consulted a medium ("witch doctor") for thirty-six years. The man's son became a minister. One day the father asked his son for a ride to the medium, even though the son had been sharing the gospel with him. The son wanted to honor his father, so he obediently gave him a ride. As the father consulted the medium, he went into a trance. The son then suggested, "Why don't you ask the medium who is the true God?" The father said, "Good idea," and asked the medium, "Who is the true God?" The medium answered, "Jesus." The father got very angry and stated, "For thirty-six years I have consulted you and paid you money, and you never told me that Jesus is the true God. Why didn't you tell me?" The medium's answer, while in a trance: "You never asked." The father subsequently turned his life over to Jesus after feeling that he had wasted much time and money.*

This story illustrates that Jesus can be found in the most unlikely places and spaces, and that we should not be surprised when people of other religions acknowledge Jesus as Lord.

Chapter 8

The Spirit's Revolution: Breaking Through the Boundaries of Superiority

Robert L. Gallagher

God sometimes speaks in surprising places and through surprising people. A few years ago, my wife, Jayna, and I were leading a group of Wheaton College undergrads in an urban immersion program to San Francisco, visiting soup kitchens, psychiatric wards, and social-welfare organizations. In the middle of the week we went to the Tenderloin district of the inner city, connecting with the homeless and listening to their stories.[1] Around noon we shared lunch with an immigrant from Honduras. He was a new arrival in the country, and since he could not find work, he was living on the streets and struggling to survive. As I listened to his story, I was surprised by his awareness of God. In our conversation over ham sandwiches I began to repeat a refrain to the stranger: "What you are saying is what Jesus said." Moreover, "What you just said is what Jesus did in the Gospels." I was stunned. The

---

[1] The Tenderloin neighborhood near downtown San Francisco encompasses fifty square blocks with a population of approximately twenty-five thousand.

foreigner was sharing that God's grace and love were available for all humanity regardless of their social status, ethnic background, or educational level. He spoke about forgiveness, acceptance, and love of all people whom the Lord brings across our path, no matter what their ideological affiliation or where they come from.

I had come to minister to the fringe community of San Francisco. Yet this homeless man was sharing spiritual truth that was breaking through my biased boundaries. God was speaking to me through this impoverished migrant as we ate lunch together. My meeting with the marginalized Latino expanded my view of the ways of the Lord. God does not confine God's purposes and grace to one set of approaches or one group of people. God works through myriad cultures and methods to accomplish divine purposes through Christ, not only within the church, but also outside the confines of the church. I set limits to what God can and should do depending on my moral, ethical, and theological boundaries. My posture is often, "God, you cannot manifest your presence and bless these people. They are not of my group or theological persuasion. And you cannot go against my theology because I am right." God desires to break down the walls that imprison our mind to demonstrate the kaleidoscopic beauty of humanity, as God's Spirit generates the fear of the Lord in the lives of people who are different from me.

WHAT'S THE PURPOSE?

In this chapter I center my attention on the relationship between two men who had a parallel experience to my Tenderloin encounter: Peter the Jewish Palestinian and Cornelius the Roman Italian. In particular, my study focuses on the spiritual intersection between the Christian Jew and the Gentile in Acts 10. Cornelius is an Italian immigrant of the Roman army, a holy man outside the realm of mission activity, and God sends an angel to honor his Gentile piety. The Lord then directs Peter to visit Cornelius, at which time the Gentile gathers his family and friends, and the Holy Spirit falls upon them. The engagement of Peter with Cornelius's household becomes a platform for Jewish Christians to participate in Gentile mission. Yet this is only half the story. Peter undergoes a theological transformation through his intersection with Cornelius as he comes to realize that "God does not show favoritism, but *accepts from every nation* the one who fears him and does what is right" (Acts 10:34–35, italics added). The Gentile Cornelius taught the Christian apostle Peter about an attribute of God that Peter did not fully understand.

Some of the questions I attempt to answer in my exploration of the Acts 10 pericope are the following: What were the boundaries or barriers between Peter and Cornelius and the reasons for them? What boundaries did God break through for this divine purpose? How did Cornelius influence Peter both directly and indirectly? Last, are there any lessons for today regarding God's desire to break through our boundaries that may be hindering the Lord's global intent? As I look at the "splinters" in Peter's view of people such as Cornelius, I am aware of the eucalyptus branches in my perceptions of humans different from myself. Thus, throughout the essay I weave my story of change as an example of God's grace in contemporary life.

The thesis of my chapter is that the mission of God not only involves God's people in prayerful trust and obedience, but also may incorporate people who are beyond the borders of the church yet whom the Lord uses to break through the boundaries established by the religious and cultural superiority of God's people. Hence, I reflect on the connections of God with Cornelius and Peter, within the Gentile-Jewish intercultural encounter, and the various ways that God brings about renovation: the alteration of Peter's view toward Gentiles, and the consequences in Cornelius's life. Finally, the chapter ends with lessons from the intercultural meeting of God with Peter and Cornelius and implications for the contemporary church.[2]

---

[2] For a consideration of my hermeneutical approach, see Robert L. Gallagher, "Transformational Teaching: Engaging in a Pneumatic Teaching Praxis," in *Thinking Theologically about Language Teaching: Christian Perspectives on an Educational Calling*, ed. Cheri L. Pierson and Will

PANORAMA PROVIDES THE MESSAGE

The author of Luke-Acts uses repeated themes to form missional tapestries throughout the writing in order to take the listener/reader on a journey of transformation as the author weaves a theological narrative through the life of Jesus and the early church. In other words, the "big sky" perspective of a biblical book allows an appropriate understanding of the first author's intent concerning a particular missional tapestry under investigation.[3]

Acts begins with the mission in Jerusalem (1:1–5:42). As the church starts to expand (6:1–9:31), the Gentile mission arises (9:32–12:25), followed by the mission to Asia Minor (present-day Turkey) and its repercussions (13:1–15:35). Beginning in Jerusalem and moving toward Europe, the gospel of Christ moves in a series of expansions shown by the changing religious categories of the people who follow the risen Lord: Galilean Jews (Acts 1), Jerusalem and diaspora Jews (Acts 2), the half-Jewish Samaritans (Acts 8), a Jewish proselyte (Acts 8), non-Jewish God-fearers

---

Bankston, 135–62 (London: Langham Global Library, 2017); idem, "Engaging in Pneumatic Mission Praxis," in *Transforming Teaching for Mission: Educational Theory and Practice*, ed. Robert A. Danielson and Benjamin L. Hartley, Association of Professors of Mission Series, 117–49 (Wilmore, KY: First Fruits Press, 2014); and idem, "Missionary Methods: St. Paul's, St. Roland's, or Ours?" in *Missionary Methods: Research, Reflection, and Realities*, ed. Craig Ott and J. D. Payne, Evangelical Missiological Society Series, no. 21, 3–22 (Pasadena, CA: William Carey Library, 2013). Also see David J. Bosch, "Reflections on Biblical Models of Mission," in *Landmark Essays in Mission and World Christianity*, ed. Robert L. Gallagher and Paul Hertig, American Society of Missiology Series, no. 43, 3–16 (Maryknoll, NY: Orbis Books, 2009).

[3] For a comprehension of the background to Acts, see Robert L. Gallagher and Paul Hertig, "Introduction: Background to Acts," in *Mission in Acts: Ancient Narratives in Contemporary Context*, ed. Robert L. Gallagher and Paul Hertig, American Society of Missiology Series, no. 34, 1–17 (Maryknoll, NY: Orbis Books, 2004). Robert C. Tannehill incorporates both Luke and Acts in his commentaries (*The Narrative Unity of Luke-Acts: A Literary Interpretation*, 2 vols. [Philadelphia: Fortress Press, 1986, 1990]).

(Acts 10—11), and non-Jewish people who have no knowledge of the Jewish faith and Hebrew scriptures (Acts 13).[4]

My interest lies with the beginning of the Gentile mission (9:32–12:25), which has four sections: Peter's mighty works (9:32–43); Cornelius's conversion (10:1–11:18); the church at Antioch of Syria (11:19–30);[5] and the imprisonment and escape of Peter (12:1–25). Since I am focusing on the conversion of Cornelius, the following four scenes are of special interest: Caesarea (10:1–8), Joppa (10:9–23a), again Caesarea (10:23b–48), and Jerusalem (11:1–18). I portray the person of Cornelius before deliberating on the journey of Peter in Luke-Acts, and the interface between the two men, together with implications for the church today.[6]

CENTURION CONQUEROR, AN ITALIAN IMMIGRANT

Before Cornelius received the Spirit of the Lord at Caesarea (10:44–46), Luke paints the portrait of a man who possesses

---

[4] For an understanding of a discourse analysis of Luke-Acts, see Robert L. Gallagher, "Luke, the Holy Spirit, and Mission: An Integrated Analysis of Selected Protestant 'Writings' in Theology, Mission, and Lukan Studies," PhD diss., Fuller Theological Seminary (1998), 10–15, 245–52.

[5] The audience of Luke-Acts would not have accepted the Christian conversion of non-Jewish people at Antioch of Syria (Acts 11) were it not for the conversion of the Gentiles at Cornelius's home first (Acts 10). The record of the Acts 10 events needed to precede the happenings at Antioch, even though Luke reverses the chronological sequence. "Now those who had been scattered by the persecution that broke out when Stephen was killed traveled as far as Phoenicia, Cyprus, and Antioch, spreading the word only among Jews. Some of them, however, men from Cyprus and Cyrene, went to [Syrian] Antioch and began to speak to Greeks [Gentiles] also, telling them the good news about the Lord Jesus. The Lord's hand was with them, and a great number of people [non-Jews] believed and turned to the Lord" (Acts 11:19–21).

[6] For the importance of reading the Bible as one story, see Michael W. Goheen, "The Biblical Story of Narrative Theology," in *Contemporary Mission Theology: Engaging the Nations*, ed. Robert L. Gallagher and Paul Hertig, American Society of Missiology Series, no. 53, 25–34 (Maryknoll, NY: Orbis Books, 2017).

unique characteristics (10:1–8). He is a powerful Italian centurion in charge of a Roman battalion (see 10:7).[7] As a European immigrant, a foreigner to the Middle East (10:28), and a high-ranking soldier of the conquering empire, we would not expect him to have any close connections with the Jewish people or their faith. He was a religious person, nevertheless, even though his army base was at Caesarea (the administrative center of the Roman occupation of Palestine), and as a professional officer of the Roman army (commanding groups of centuries of two hundred to one thousand legionaries), he forced peace upon the war-ravaged state.[8]

The writer of Acts describes Cornelius as a religiously devout person who feared God with his entire household (10:2, 35). His devotion influenced his servants, fellow soldiers, and Gentile family to follow the Jewish God (10:2, 7, 24; 11:14).[9] As a Gentile God-fearer or God-worshiper, he regularly attended the local synagogue to worship the one, true, living God by participating in the liturgy from the assigned seating in the back row.[10] Unlike a proselyte, such as the Ethiopian eunuch (8:27), he did not embrace circumcision (Gen 17:9–14), yet he did observe the Sabbath and the food laws (Lev 11:1–47). God-fearers worshiped

---

[7] The author of Luke-Acts also mentions the Roman military presence in Luke 3:14; 7:1–10; Acts 21:31; 23:10, 16–35; 24:24—25:5; 26:30–32; 27:1.

[8] For an understanding of Roman Caesarea, see A. B. Spencer, "Caesarea Maritima," in *Major Cities of the Biblical World*, ed. R. K. Harrison (Nashville, TN: Thomas Nelson Publishers, 1985), 63–71; and James S. Jeffers, *The Greco-Roman World of the New Testament Era: Exploring the Background of Early Christianity* (Downers Grove, IL: InterVarsity Press, 1999), 123–30.

[9] See references in Acts to entire households converting to God: 10:2; 16:15, 31–34; 18:8; see Lk 7:2.

[10] Other instances of Luke mentioning God-fearing Gentiles are in Acts 10:22, 35; 13:16, 26, 43; 16:14; 17:4, 17; 18:7. Paul found the God-fearers particularly receptive to the gospel of the Lord Jesus (Acts 13:42–43).

the monotheistic Jewish God and followed the ethical and moral code of the faith.[11]

Luke describes Cornelius, furthermore, as a generous person in deeds of charity toward the Jewish people, together with praying to God continually (10:2, 35; see Lk 7:4–5). His devotion to prayer implies that he followed the daily prayer regime of the Jewish faith (cf. Acts 3:1; Dan 6:10).[12] During one of his prayer sessions God gave the Roman a vision of a holy angel speaking to him, saying, "Your prayers and gifts to the poor have come up as a memorial offering before God" (10:4; cf. 10:31). Later in the chapter Luke reinforces Cornelius's character by declaring that he was a righteous and God-fearing man, well spoken of by the entire Jewish nation (10:22; cf. Lk 7:4–5). Cornelius the holy man, though, is outside the realm of the church's mission activity. Yet God sends an angel in a vision to honor his Gentile piety.

PETER'S ROAD TRIP IN LUKE-ACTS

Luke positions Cornelius, the righteous Gentile, alongside Peter, the righteous Messianic Jew. The difference between the men lies in their power and control. The Roman soldier has a militarist authority and political power over the Palestinian apostle. Yet, ironically, when first meeting Peter, Cornelius humbly bows in reverence before the church leader (10:25–26; cf. Lk 7:6–8). Conversely, the Jewish people had no power or authority over

---

[11] J. A. Overman supports this traditional understanding of the "God-fearers" ("The God-fearers: Some Neglected Features," *Journal for the Study of the New Testament* 32, no. 1 [1988]: 17–26). Also see J. Julius Scott, Jr., *Customs and Controversies: Intertestamental Jewish Backgrounds of the New Testament* (Grand Rapids, MI: Baker Books, 1995), 342–47.

[12] For the daily office or fixed–hour prayer, see I. Howard Marshall, *The Acts of the Apostles: An Introduction and Commentary*, Tyndale New Testament Commentaries (Grand Rapids, MI: Eerdmans, [1980] 2001), 184–85.

the Italian army. Yet, for nearly fifteen years after Pentecost (Acts 2), the messianic believers had exercised control over the good news of Christ and built boundaries of spiritual superiority that thwarted Gentile God-worshipers from receiving the full blessing of God's Messiah.[13]

Sitting between Bookends of Bigotry

Like Peter, we have similar constructs that form emotional boundaries in our minds, which then prevent people from receiving God's fullness in Christ. After working twenty years in an Australian industrial city, I became an immigrant as I moved my family to Pasadena, California, to study at Fuller Theological Seminary. In the fall of 1990 my first class was Christian anthropology. The professor spent the beginning of the course challenging the superiority of the West by comparing the majority world with respect to issues of family, morals, and ethics. This approach disturbed many of my Western colleagues, who felt that the leveling of their society and the uplifting of other world cultures was inappropriate. After five weeks of the course I had considered all my possible biases and superiorities toward other people groups. By measuring my journey from small-town monoculturalism to the multiculturalism of an immigrant city—first as a materials engineer in a steel works, then as a high school teacher at a Catholic school, and finally as an executive pastor among a congregation of over fifty cultures—the conclusion I reached was that I was not prejudiced. I did not have any unfairness that would hinder me in connecting and ministering with people of another ethnicity. I even decided that if my family stayed in the United States, I would be at peace

---

[13] I believe that Pentecost in Acts 2 occurred in 30 CE, and that the events of Acts 10 were around 48 CE with the Council of Jerusalem in 49 CE (Acts 15). For the dates of Acts, see F. F. Bruce, *The Acts of the Apostles: The Greek Text with Introduction and Commentary* (Grand Rapids, MI: Eerdmans, [1951] 1968), 10–14.

if my two daughters (who at the time were nine and twelve years of age) married men from North America.

Consequently, I sat comfortably in an auditorium at Fuller Seminary on the sixth week of the course between two men who, in the pressure-cooker milieu of graduate studies, had become close friends. The professor had changed his trajectory in the class and was expanding on another topic, when suddenly into my mind came two television-type pictures, both involving my mother. Now, I need to say that my mother was and is a gracious person; when you meet her in heaven, you will agree to her godly character. Nonetheless, since I was the youngest child of three (my two siblings were already in college before I uttered my first words), my mother would tell me the oral history of our family by repeating the stories of her early marriage. It was two stories from my mother's history lessons that invaded my thoughts that morning in class.

The first image concerned me as a five-year-old holding my mother's hand, walking along the main street of our town. When I saw a candy on the ground and reached down to pick it up, my mom yanked my hand and spoke a cautionary proverb. The phrase she unconsciously uttered originated in the Australian gold fields of the 1860s and regarded the Chinese people. It was not a sympathetic utterance since it related to matters of hygiene. A split second later came the other image of my mother telling me another story. The occasion of this narrative came from the days when my parents were teaching in far-western New South Wales at a one-classroom elementary school in a one-store town. The people who owned the grocery store were from the subcontinent of India, and they had rice barrels on the porch. In order to push down the rice, the owner would take off his shoes and tread in the barrels, squashing the rice down to make room for more product. My mother again expressed horror at the unhygienic nature of the procedure. That morning at Fuller Seminary the Holy Spirit brought to my mind these two pictures of my mom speaking to me as a young boy.

There I sat on my cushioned chair between two colleagues in a seminary classroom, smugly assured of my lack of paternalism and prejudice toward other peoples, when the Spirit brought to my attention my superior enculturations. Somehow, through my upbringing, I had inherited a narrow-mindedness of which I was oblivious. On my right sat a Chinese pastor from Singapore; on the other side, an Indian evangelist from the United Kingdom. Sitting between the bookends of my bigotry, I spoke of my experience to my Chinese friend and repented of my suppressed feelings. He smiled and responded, "That's nothing. You should hear what we say about you." Similar to the apostle Peter, I travel along a rocky road as the Spirit of God continues to align my twisted enculturations with God's desired will.

Peter's Broken Road to Jerusalem

We need to examine Peter's attitude toward non-Jewish people in the Gospels to comprehend his revolutionary road trip from his monocultural prejudice to an awareness of God's cross-cultural kingdom perspective. It is in the Gospels that we see evidence of God's patience in shifting the apostle's thinking away from his Jewish, first-century boundaries and toward God's love of all nations. Peter's progressive understanding of God's heart for the Gentiles slowly trickles through the influence of Jesus's teaching and actions.

The attitude of some first-century Jewish people toward non-Jewish people was one of superiority. Consequently, on a number of occasions Peter and the disciples display discrimination toward Gentiles, even in the midst of Jesus's actions and teaching that demonstrate the inclusion of Gentiles in the kingdom of God.[14]

---

[14] See Luke 9:52–56; cf. John 4:19–21. Even among their own band, there existed pride, arrogance, and supremacy. "Who is the greatest among us?" is a constant chorus. The Gospels repeat this motif on a number of occasions, indicating that the question of who is the greatest in the kingdom was an important issue to the followers of Jesus (see Mt 18:1–6; Mk 9:33–37; Lk 9:46–48). Sadly, Jesus's followers even discussed

Jesus, the Cross-cultural Worker

Peter witnessed displays of Jesus's compassion toward Gentiles such as the deliverance of Legion at Gerasenes (Mk 5:1–20); the healing of the deaf and dumb person in the region of the Decapolis (Mk 7:31–37); and Jesus teaching in Magadan (Mt 15:39), Tyre (Mk 7:31), Dalmanutha (Mk 8:1), and beyond the Jordan (Mk 10:1). These regions displayed little ethnic resemblance to the monoculturalism of Judea. Jesus's good deeds to non-Jewish people and regions intruded upon Peter's boundaries of superiority by demonstrating God's borderless love of all humanity.[15]

Jesus's Narrative Twist

Not only did the Lord Jesus change his followers' perceptions of the kingdom of God by his restorative actions toward non-Israelites, but he also taught on the issue. In Matthew 8:1–13 and Luke 13:22–30, God invites people beyond the ethnic family of Israel to feast at the banquet table of eternal fellowship. Others of those outside the insider's group will likewise eat at the Lord's feast, sitting alongside the venerable patriarchs of old: Abraham, Isaac, and Jacob. In the teaching of Jesus, furthermore, he throws in a narrative twist by claiming that those who are smugly at ease, sitting on their preconceived divine right as children of the kingdom, will find themselves eternally separated from the God they are allegedly following.

---

which of them was the greatest during the last supper (Lk 22:24–30). Their attitude contrasted with the Son of God, who was among them to serve and not to lord his authority over them (Jn 13:12–17). Christ endeavored to break through the boundaries of his followers' superiority by comparing the correct posture in God's kingdom with the attitude of a child (Lk 9:47–48).

[15] Cf. Luke 7:1–10 and the healing of the centurion's servant; and Matthew 15:21–28 on the deliverance of the Canaanite's daughter. For an understanding of multicultural Galilee, see Paul Hertig, "The Multi-ethnic Journeys of Jesus in Matthew: Margin-Center Dynamics," *Missiology: An International Review* 26, no. 1 (1998): 23–35.

The upside-down kingdom has struck again. Who, then, can be sure of the way of salvation? Jesus repeatedly breaks through the theological boundaries that limit God's kingdom to a select ethnic or religious group. The Lord thus turned the sacred boundaries inside out.[16] Jesus designed these judgment oracles to motivate the Jewish listeners toward repentance so that they would be sitting at the king's banquet alongside the Gentile faithful.[17]

Peeling Back Layers of Prejudice

God also led me along a pathway of repentance following my experience sitting between my "bookends" of bias at Fuller Seminary. The Lord began to peel back layers of prejudice that I had suppressed beneath the surface of my conscious thoughts: unchallenged feelings of chauvinism toward those whom God

---

[16] The teaching of the Lord Jesus should not have been outlandish to Jewish ears. The Hebrew scriptures echo his instructions when it declares that the God of all the earth, the Ruler and King of the nations, shall bring forth springs of salvation among all peoples so that God's name will be great among the nations and known throughout all the earth (see Is 12:4–5; 54:5; Jer 10:6–7; Mal 1:11). To use another Old Testament metaphor, God desires the chosen people to be a light for the nations to bring salvation to the end of the earth (see Is 42:6; 49:6; 51:4; 60:1, 3; cf. Lk 2:32; 13:47; 26:23). In fact, Jesus during his Temple thrashing in Mark 11:17, proclaims Isaiah 56:7, that the Temple is "a house of prayer for all nations" (see Jer 7:11; Mt 21:13; Lk 19:46).

[17] In particular, the theological illustrations of Jesus often promote the marginalized of Jewish society such as the Samaritans, tax-collectors, women, and the poor. The woman at the well of Sychar in Samaria (Jn 4:1–42) is an early evangelist and interpreter of theological truth. In the parable of Luke 10:25–37, a Samaritan shows mercy toward his Jewish enemy and teaches all Israel how to inherit eternal life. Moreover, Jesus requested hospitality of Zacchaeus, the chief tax-collector of Jericho, and declared that salvation had come to his house as a son of Abraham (Lk 19:1–10). In addition, the Jericho thief (19:8) was one of four rich men in Luke's Gospel, and the only one who receives salvation (cf. Lk 12:13–21; 16:19–31; 18:18–25).

should not seat at his banqueting table. Similar to an onion being peeled back, layer by layer, God began to reveal my biases, which were foolish and lacked rational explanation. We are all on a spiritual journey, and many of us are on a road trip from monoculturalism toward God's intercultural outlook.

As a child, my first prejudice concerned males. For instance, a man walks into a room immaculately dressed in a suit, tie, and dress shoes. As he sits on a chair, I notice that he is wearing white socks. Immediately I presuppose that I am superior to him. I put him in a pigeonhole where I am above him in all respects. I am ten years old. I do not know his character, morality, educational background, or profession. I understand nothing at all about him. Yet I believe that I am superior to him. Where did that warped predisposition come from?

The next illustration concerns my inequity toward females. I am still ten years old and know absolutely zero about sexuality. I see a woman walking toward me, and she has pierced ears. She has pierced ears with dangling earrings. Instantly I am a wealth of ignorant understanding and place her in another slot of prejudgment. To my young mind she is obviously a woman of loose morals, a licentious woman who could effortlessly bat her eyelashes and seduce men to their destruction (see Prov 6:25). What could a woman with pierced ears possibly mean to an eighty-pound boy who is less than five feet tall? How did these thoughts evolve? Where did those attitudes come from?

I recognize that my parents did not sit me down as a little boy and warn me of the inferiority of men who wear white socks, or for that matter, the promiscuity of women who had holes in their ears. My world was shattered one afternoon when my seventy-year-old mother entered our home with pierced ears and wearing dainty pearl earrings. God pushed me to adjust my preconception as I gradually endured a cognitive paradigm shift. Analogous to the Lord's dealings with Peter in Luke-Acts, God began breaking through the boundaries of my prejudice against his multifaceted humanity during these accumulated experiences.

Peter's Rocky Road to Rome

The apostle Peter's continuing road trip across the book of Acts still needed God's patience and a variety of methods to bring him closer to the Lord's ideal, even though the early disciple had witnessed Jesus's healing and deliverance of non-Jews and had heard a clear pronouncement that the Gentiles were included in God's kingdom. As we observe Peter's movement from monocultural to cross-cultural awareness within Acts, the boundaries of religious superiority slowly break down over time.[18]

In Acts 2, Peter's commentary of Joel 2 included correlating the supernatural manifestations of Pentecost with the declaration that everyone who calls on the name of God shall be saved (2:21; cf. Joel 2:32). No longer is Yahweh saving his people from physical peril, as in the time of Joel, but Peter uses the Hebrew prophet to proclaim the present salvation of the nations through the divine Lord Jesus. I doubt whether Peter fully comprehended the significance of his spiritual claim. Yet he underscores this point again in Acts 3:25 by quoting Genesis 12:3 in referring to all nations being blessed through the Messiah Jesus, and with another illusion to the same issue in Acts 4:24 (Gal 3:8; cf. Gen 22:18; 26:4; 28:14).

Cracks continue to appear in the apostle's boundaries of spiritual superiority,[19] so much so that Peter eventually accepts the hospitality of Simon the tanner, who lives beside the sea at Joppa (9:43; cf. 10:5, 32). Simon lives some distance from the city because of the pungent odors of his industry, and by the ocean to use the salt water to clean the carcasses of dead animals to make hides for such commodities as tents.[20] According to Jewish law, Peter's friend is ceremonially unclean because he is perpetually

---

[18] At the end of all four Gospels, Jesus in his resurrection teaching made it clear that the kingdom of God would include non-Jewish people and that his followers would be used to bring in the Gentile harvest (Mt 28:16–20; Mk 16:14–18; Lk 24:44–49; Jn 20:19–23; cf. Acts 1:8).

[19] In Acts 8:17, Peter experiences the coming of the Holy Spirit to the half-Jewish nation of the Samaritans.

[20] Paul was also a leatherworker or tentmaker (Acts 18:3; cf. 20:34).

gutting the internal organs of dead animals (Lev 11:39–40).[21] At this juncture of the apostle's travels he has broken through the impurity boundaries that isolated the religiously unclean professionals from regular friendship and table fellowship (9:43; see Num 19:22). In the next section I examine the episode that launches Peter's informed recognition of God's cross-cultural perspective, in which the Gentile nations have complete access to the Messiah's kingdom.

THE SPIRIT'S REVOLUTION

At the beginning of Acts 10, the scene shifts from Joppa and the relationship with Peter and Simon to Caesarea and Peter's association with Cornelius. As we have seen, the Roman soldier is a devout God-fearer whose prayers and charity the Lord recognized. While practicing fixed-hour prayer at three in the afternoon, the migrant receives a vision of an angel giving him directions to contact Simon Peter, who is staying with his friend by the sea at Joppa, and bring him back to Caesarea. Cornelius was afraid when he first saw the angel. Yet, when the vision finished, the centurion (after explaining the supernatural visitation to two of his house servants and a loyal soldier), sends the party to Joppa to bring Peter back to his home (10:1–8; cf. 11:13).[22]

---

[21] For an understanding of how Jewish people considered Simon the tanner's occupation as unclean, see John Stott, *The Message of Acts: The Spirit, the Church, and World* (Downers Grove, IL: InterVarsity Press, 1990), 184.

[22] vanThanh Nguyen uses the narrative-critical method in biblical studies to show the social context and theological significance of the episode with Peter and Cornelius (see *Peter and Cornelius: A Story of Conversion and Mission*, American Society of Missiology Monograph Series, vol. 15 [Eugene, OR: Pickwick Publications, 2012]). A missional study of the incident is also found in Denton Lotz, "Peter's Wider Understanding of God's Will: Acts 10:34–48," *International Review of Missions* 77, no. 3 (1988): 201–7. For a sociocultural study of Cornelius, see E. A. Judge, *Social Distinctives of the Christians in the First Century* (Peabody, MA: Hendrickson Publishers, 2008), 24–25.

The Spirit Presses the Boundaries

As the Cornelius group approaches the city of Joppa, Peter, who is also practicing fixed-hour prayer at noon, falls into a trance on the housetop and sees a vision, not of an angel, but of a conglomeration of non-Jewish food. It was lunch time, and his host was preparing a meal. Peter becomes famished, smelling the delicious kosher aromas wafting up from the kitchen below. In the heat of the midday sun—after enduring many days of the foul stench of rotting flesh and stinking carcasses tinged with salt spray—Peter is overcome with pangs of hunger. In a vision displayed three times, he sees a huge sheet lowered from heaven to earth tied at its four corners and occupied by all types of wild animals, reptiles, and birds; and three times God speaks to him saying, "Get up, Peter. Kill and eat." And each time Peter responds, "Surely not, Lord! I have never eaten anything impure or unclean." Again, three times God answers, "Do not call anything impure that God has made clean." The meaning of the vision perplexes Peter (10:9–16; cf. 11:4–10).

Meanwhile, the band from Caesarea had found the home of the tanner on the outskirts of the city and called out for Peter from the gate. While the apostle was still thinking about the meaning of the vision, the Holy Spirit declared that three men were looking for him and that he was to go with them without question because the Spirit had sent them. After Peter introduces himself to the trio, he hears of the righteous Cornelius and his angelic visitation. He then extends hospitality to the Gentile visitors to stay the night and presumably to eat with him and his tanner host (10:17–23a; cf. 11:11–12a).

The Spirit Pushes the Boundaries

The following day the party sets out for Caesarea, thirty-five miles north of Joppa, a journey of two days on foot along the coastal road (10:24a). On their arrival at Caesarea, six Jewish men accompanying Peter, as well as the returning Gentile group, enter the Roman courtyard (11:12). The Gentile centurion prostrates himself in reverence before the Jew. After Peter lifts him up, the apostle announces to those assembled: "You are well aware that it is against our law for a Jew to associate with or visit a Gentile. *But God has shown me that I should not call anyone impure or unclean.* So when I was sent for, I came without raising any objection. May I ask why you sent for me?" (Acts 10:28–29, italics added).[23] In the tripartite proclamation Peter first confesses that he has never had any association with non-Jewish people. He asserts, "You are well aware that it is against our law for a Jew to associate with or visit a Gentile." This implies that he has never entered a Gentile home and therefore has never eaten nonkosher food with non-Jewish people, an acknowledgment of what he had said to God three times during his trance: "Lord, I have never eaten anything unholy or unclean." In other words, he had always obeyed God's covenantal rules regarding his association with Gentiles (10:14). Until this moment the Christian religious leader had never had any association with non-Jewish people, conveniently forgetting his overnight connections with the Cornelius entourage. Why did Peter feel the necessity for such a pronouncement when he knew that the gathered Gentiles already were aware of the Jewish restrictions (10:28a)? Was the first disciple speaking primarily to himself and his six companions, underscoring the significance of the moment because he knew the consequences of his actions would reverberate around the walls of the church?

In answer to Peter's question of why Cornelius had asked him to come to Caesarea, the centurion reiterates the story of his angelic visitation (10:30–33). The apostle responds by expanding the perception of his Joppa vision, which he first articulated in 10:28b: "I now realize how true it is that *God does not show favoritism, but accepts from every nation* [Jew and Gentile] the one who fears him and does what is right. You know the message God sent to the people of Israel, announcing the good news of

---

[23] F. F. Bruce asserts, "The first words that Peter spoke were words of the weightiest import, sweeping away the racial and religious prejudices of centuries" (*The Book of Acts*, rev. ed. [Grand Rapids, MI: Eerdmans, 1988], 211).

peace through *Jesus Christ, who is Lord of all* [Jew and Gentile]" (10:34b–36, italics added).

Peter continues by telling the history of Jesus of Nazareth: empowered by the Holy Spirit in ministry, put to death, and raised by God (10:37–42); with his followers now bearing witness that "*everyone who believes in him* receives forgiveness of sins through his name" (10:43, italics added). Peter's third interpretation of his vision of creatures great and small is the declaration that through the name of Jesus there is forgiveness of sins for everyone (both Jew and Gentile) who believes. While Peter was still speaking, the Holy Spirit fell upon everyone in the room, astonishing the Messianic Jews "because the gift of the Holy Spirit had been poured out even on Gentiles. For they heard them speaking in tongues and praising God" (10:44–47; cf. 11:15–18; 15:7–11). After yet another change of perspective, Peter baptized the Gentile believers (10:47; cf. 11:17) and remained with them for a few days accepting their table fellowship (10:44–48; cf. 11:3). The Holy Spirit worked sovereignly and unexpectedly beyond Jewish-Gentile boundaries. The hospitality of Gentiles welcoming Jewish Christians into their home laid the foundation for the continuing revolutionary work of the Holy Spirit.[24]

The Early Church and the Law

When the news escaped throughout Judea that the Gentiles had received the word of God, the reaction in Jerusalem indicates a prevailing belief that some early Christians held and that they believed Peter should embrace. "The apostles and the believers throughout Judea heard that the Gentiles also had received the word of God. So when Peter went up to Jerusalem, the circumcised believers criticized him and said, '*You went into the house of uncircumcised men and*

---

[24] Bruce contends, "As in Peter's vision, the voice of God overruled food restrictions, even those imposed with the authority of divine law, so now the act of God in sending the Spirit overruled the sacred tradition, which forbade association with Gentiles" (*The Book of Acts*, 217).

ate with them'" (11:1–3, italics added).[25] In the early church there was an influential group of Christians who insisted on the full observance of the Mosaic Law, including circumcision, for those who believed in the Messiah.[26] These ultraconservatives clashed with Peter when he came to Jerusalem (11:2–18). The Judaist Christians, in particular, targeted the religious boundary of food restrictions that God had broken through. Jewish custom forbade eating and drinking with non-Jewish people because the association would pollute the purity of the Jewish followers. God is pure and holy, and if any Jewish believers connected with an impure Gentile, then their ceremonial purity was contaminated, and they would have to undergo purification rites before entering God's presence again (Mt 15:2; Mk 7:1–6, 14–23; Lk 11:37–41; Jn 2:6; 3:25).[27]

---

[25] In the early church there were four views of the law: (1) Full observance of the Mosaic Law, including circumcision. The "circumcised believers" demanded that Gentiles had to become Jews (Acts 11:2; Gal 2:4). (2) No circumcision required, but some Jewish observances, especially the Jewish food laws (Acts 15:20; 18:18; 21:17–26; Gal 2:12). Peter belonged to this moderately conservative Christian group that agreed with Paul that the church should not impose circumcision on the Gentiles. In Antioch of Syria, Paul opposed Peter face to face and separated with Barnabas over this issue (Gal 2:11, 13; cf. Acts 21:20–26). (3) No circumcision and no food laws (1 Cor 8:1–13; Gal 3:10–13, 23–29, esp. 24–25; cf. Gal 2:11, 13). (4) No circumcision, no food laws, and no abiding significance in Jewish worship and feasts (Jn 2:19–21; 4:21; 5:1, 9b; 6:4; 7:2; 10:34; 15:25).

[26] "Then some of the believers who belonged to the party of the Pharisees stood up and said, 'The Gentiles must be circumcised and required to keep the law of Moses'" (Acts 15:5).

[27] For an appreciation of first-century Jewish purity issues, see Acts 21:23–26; 24:18; cf. John 11:55; 18:18. Also see Joachim Jeremias, *Jerusalem in the Times of Jesus: An Investigation into Economic and Social Conditions during the New Testament Period* (Philadelphia: Fortress Press, 1969), 270–358; Bruce J. Malina, *The New Testament World: Insights from Cultural Anthropology*, rev. ed. (Louisville, KY: Westminster/John Knox Press, 1993), 149–83; and Jerome H. Neyrey, "Ceremonies in Luke-Acts: The Case of Meals and Table Fellowship," in *The Social World of Luke-Acts: Models for Interpretation*, ed. Jerome H. Neyrey (Peabody, MA: Hendrickson Publishers, 1991), 361–87.

Peter's announcement of the theological watershed was more for the apostle and his Jewish companions than for Cornelius and the Gentiles gathered at Caesarea (see Acts 10:28). The church of Acts was soaked in ages of superiority, and the barrels were about to burst with the new wine of acceptance flowing into Gentile wineskins, which would expand the gospel into non-Jewish territory (cf. Mk 2:22). Perhaps Peter remembered the words of Jesus on their first meeting when the Lord told the Galilean that he would no longer be catching fish but catching people for God's kingdom (Mk 1:16–18). Now the revelation comes to Peter that Jesus was talking about catching Jewish *and* Gentile people in the net of God's care and concern. The apostle's long journey of adjustment to God's way of thinking is about to end; he underscores the significance of the moment to himself and his Jewish comrades.[28]

THE SPIRIT'S BOUNDARY BREAKERS

Peter's second assertion of Acts 10:28–29 is the statement to the non-Jewish assembly: "But God has shown me that I should not call anyone impure or unclean." What has happened in Peter's mind between Joppa and Caesarea to shift him from puzzling over the vision to this revolutionary declaration (10:17a, 19a)? How did God show him? What were the means of God's revelation? Before considering the immediate causes of the Lord's disclosure, we need to realize that Peter's movement was riveted

---

[28] For the theological and missiological significance of the event for the life and mission of the church, see Charles E. Van Engen, "Peter's Conversion: A Culinary Disaster Launches the Gentile Mission," in Gallagher and Hertig, *Mission in Acts*, 133–43. Also see Ajith Fernando, *Acts*, NIV Application Commentary (Grand Rapids, MI: Zondervan, 1998), 270–85; Justo L. González, *Acts: The Gospel of the Spirit* (Maryknoll, NY: Orbis Books, 2001), 130–36; and Jaroslav Pelikan, *Acts*, Brazos Theological Commentary on the Bible (Grand Rapids, MI: Brazos Press, 2005), 128–36.

in his accrued experiences of Jesus's words and deeds (Lk 24:47; Acts 1:6, 8), the Spirit's revelation in Jerusalem (Acts 2:21; 3:25; 4:24), the Samaritan believers' receiving the Holy Spirit (Acts 8:17), and his friendship with Simon the leatherworker (Acts 9:43).

God shadowed these actions through the following direct boundary breakers to complete the paradigmatic swing in Peter's thinking: the directing angel of Cornelius's vision; dialoguing with God in a vision; God's guiding voice; showing hospitality toward the Caesarea band; resolving tensions at Cornelius's home; expressing the truth of the Lord Jesus; experiencing the Spirit upon the Gentiles; opposition concerning water baptism, circumstances aligning; communicating to believers in conflict; and comparing the historic precedent of Pentecost. The accumulated effect of these boundary breakers shattered the walls of Peter's superiority to such an extent that the disciple's vision of the kingdom was never the same again, and the church was thrust into a new direction, never to return to the old road of tradition. In the succeeding segment I expand only the first two of these boundary breakers because of the limited scope of the chapter.

Cornelius's Vision

Before Peter experienced the events surrounding Cornelius, he was present when Jesus reached across bigotry to another centurion and affirmed, "I have not seen such great faith in all of Israel." Peter was there when Jesus delivered the demon from the daughter of the Syro-Phoenician woman, empowering the family with human dignity. Yet by Acts 10, Peter had never entered a Gentile home and, consequently, never eaten non-Jewish food. The apostle's attitudinal transformation toward the non-Jewish people took nearly twenty years of close relationship with Jesus and his Spirit. Therefore, what finally convinced Peter at Caesarea that these happenings were of God? Moreover, what persuaded the ultraconservative Christians in Jerusalem that the Lord was orchestrating the proceedings?[29]

The first stimulus in the breaking of Peter's boundaries was the vision of Cornelius. The writer of Acts archives five accounts of the angel speaking to Cornelius. The first instance was the historical encounter of the angel of God in the vision at Caesarea (10:3–6). The second occasion occurred when the centurion retold the story to his two servants and a God-fearing soldier who was one of his attendants (10:7–8). Cornelius told the story without any details noted. "He told them everything that had happened and sent them to Joppa." Next, the three men retold the account to Peter, adding that the angel was "holy" and that Peter was to come to their master's house "so that he could hear what you have to say" (10:21–23a). The fourth occurrence was Cornelius retelling the incident to Peter at Caesarea. For the first time, Luke has the Roman praying in his house and stating, "A man in shining clothes stood before me." This is the second time that Cornelius told the story. The remembrance and directions of the angel are the same, except for the supplement of Peter being a guest in Simon's home (10:29b–32). Fifth, the Jerusalem leaders hear Peter retelling the story that Cornelius told him with the additional commentary of the angel's communication: "He will bring you a message through which you and all your household will be saved" (cf. 10:22c).

Peter, after a number of days of reflection (cf. 10:48b; 11:2a), concluded the proceedings with his understanding of God's ultimate purpose: the salvation of the Gentiles through the Spirit of Jesus.[30] The angel said, "He [Peter] will bring you [Cornelius] a message through which you and all your household will be saved" (11:14). This completed Peter's third time in hearing the story:

---

[29] Bruce describes how Peter's vision (with the work of the Holy Spirit) is the crucial action of God in moving the Jewish church to accept the Gentile mission (*The Book of Acts*, 222–23).

[30] For the Lukan view of God reaching out to the Gentiles with salvation, see Robert L. Gallagher, "Good News for All People: Engaging Luke's Narrative Soteriology of the Nations," in Gallagher and Hertig, *Contemporary Mission Theology*, 193–202.

the servants in Joppa, Cornelius in Caesarea, and now his own rendition in Jerusalem.

Why are there so many references to the vision of Cornelius? Certainly, the repetition is for a literary purpose, as is the reiteration of the entire story at Caesarea, Joppa, Caesarea (again), and Jerusalem. Conceivably, the fivefold pattern underscores that God was arranging the proceedings and not human beings, which serves the same purpose for Peter in his triple storytelling encounter. The duplication drew attention to the revolutionary character of the changes that were unfolding. God was speaking to and directing the Gentiles. Most important, God used the repeated story of a Gentile to lay the foundation for the transformation of a Jew. In addition, the guidance of the Lord in the angel-vision combination was a continuation of the providence of God in the Hebrew scriptures and early church. These events were a part of the enduring economy of God, which the first-century church knew and did not consider bizarre.[31]

Peter's Vision

Another means that God used in dislodging Peter from his preconceived notions was the thrice-repeated vision of the animal-filled sheet, together with God's beckoning him to eat, Peter's refusal, and God's voice speaking to him again: "Do not call anything impure that God has made clean." Each of these sections occurs three times. The day that God chose to invade

---

[31] References to angels and/or visions as God's guidance in both the Old Testament and early church are numerous. For example, the visions of Acts 9:10, 12; 10:3, 17, 19; 11:5; 16:9–10; 18:9–10; 26:19. Both Peter and Paul fell into a trance and saw a vision (Acts 10:10; 11:5; 22:17). What is the difference between a trance and a vision? Luke uses different terminology, but they are the same phenomenon (cf. 26:19). Further, the Peter-Paul parallelism is a literary device to display the apostolic authority of Paul, since he was not one of the original apostles. Examples of angels are in Luke 1:11; 2:9; Acts 5:19; 8:26; 12:7–11, 23; 10:3; 27:23; cf. Mt 1:20, 24; 2:13, 19; 28:2.

Peter's worldview was an ordinary day. He was following his daily prayer pattern on the housetop, possibly praying Jewish liturgy (1:14; 2:42; 3:1; 6:4) and/or Hebrew texts regarding the Messiah that he knew had come to pass (cf. 4:24–30). Years after the birth of the church at Pentecost, Peter was still following Jewish rituals of prayer.

Certainly there was a connection between Peter wanting to eat lunch and the vision enticing him to eat unclean foods. God joined the natural impulses of the man together with the Lord's divine purposes. Further, the Lord linked smells, sights, and sounds to forge the memory of the experience into the disciple's psyche. For days, a variety of odors, views, and noises had blanketed Peter in prayer on the rooftop overlooking the Mediterranean. Each time he had suffered the overpowering odor of decaying animal bodies with wafts of sea spray bringing temporary relief. Shrilling birds shattered the hollow sounds of the sea patrolling the beach. And the pitiless sun bounced its fire off the raging waters.

On that unique day God disturbed Peter's normalcy. In a trance—instead of observing the sea, beach, and clouds—he looked up and saw a celestial vision. The drifting aromas of the midday meal were interrupted by the foul stench of despised beasts that he could not tolerate, all scurrying about on a massive sheet; the offensive creatures were interrupting the sounds of surf and sand with alarming noises that were foreign to Peter's ears (see Lev 11:1–47). The invasion of smells, sights, and sounds disgusting to the orthodox Jew became distressing. As was the Lord's intent, Peter would never forget this designed event. God had marinated the vision with primordial vexations that bruised the five senses.[32]

---

[32] Peter and Paul both experienced trances with accompanying visions (Acts 10:10; 11:5; 22:17). They were praying, then in a trance saw a vision, and debated audibly with God (see 10:14; 22:19–20). Peter remained puzzled because there was no interpretation, while Paul instantly obeyed, God having given him a clear directive (10:17; 22:21). Cornelius in his vision also received specific details: "Now send men to Joppa to bring back a man named Simon who is called Peter. He is staying with Simon the tanner, whose house is by the sea" (10:5–6). Likewise, the vision of Ananias of Damascus was precise: "The Lord told him, 'Go to the house

Peter, standing before the crowd in Cornelius's apartments, concluded that God had cleansed the nations. He finally comprehended the linkage between the creatures on the sheet and God's announcement concerning the people of all nations: "Do not call anything impure that God has made clean." God used the nonkosher animals as a metaphor to represent nonkosher people. The unclean animals were not the issue. The Jewish view of unclean humans was at the center of the divine concern. Jesus had declared all foods clean, and now Peter's vision extrapolated this concept to include all peoples.[33]

IN THE END

In the contemporary world we are not alone with our bigotries and intolerances. The scriptures surround us with a cloud of witnesses whose lives are shouting forth abuses of superiority. For instance, my case study of the apostle Peter—one of the inner circle of Jesus's entourage, the rock upon whom God builds the church, and to whom the Lord Jesus gave the keys of the kingdom (Mt 16:13–20)—proves that point. I have taken you on a road trip with Peter through the Gospels and the book of Acts. During the journey I observed the events that brought about a paradigmatic change in his perspective from monoculturalism to God's cross-culturalism—in other words, a transformation from believing that

---

of Judas on Straight Street and ask for a man from Tarsus named Saul, for he is praying. In a vision he has seen a man named Ananias come and place his hands on him to restore his sight'" (9:11–12). Similar to the vision of Peter, Ananias argues with the Lord concerning the directive before obeying (9:13–19).

[33] "Do not defile yourselves by any of these creatures. Do not make yourselves unclean by means of them or be made unclean by them. I am the Lord your God; consecrate yourselves and be holy, because I am holy. Do not make yourselves unclean by any creature that moves along the ground. I am the Lord, who brought you up out of Egypt to be your God; therefore be holy, because I am holy" (Lev 11:43–45). See Leviticus 22:1–3 for an Israelite to be ceremonially unclean and cut off from God's presence.

God is only for the Jewish people to a realignment of God as the Lord of all peoples, tribes, tongues, and nations (Rev 5:9–10).

In the case of Peter and Cornelius, God is the orchestrator of the revolutionary events as the Lord guides "Peter to use the keys of the kingdom to open a 'door of faith' to Gentiles."[34] Yet, the Lord arranges the visions for both Gentile and Jewish Christian, but in such a manner that the men only receive a part of the picture of God's purpose. It is only when they listen to each other's story of their visionary experiences that the Holy Spirit reveals to Peter that all the nations are being accepted into Christ's kingdom, and the Spirit comes upon the Gentile God-fearers as proof that they indeed belong to the church of Jesus Christ. The two men need each other to embrace the fullness of God's intent. The text in Acts 10 provides biblical proof of God's inclusion of Gentiles as missionaries to the Lord's people, and vice versa, the presence of God's people as cross-cultural workers to the non-Jewish nations.

My overarching thesis is that throughout salvation history the Lord consistently teaches God's people and expands the kingdom by means of individuals from outside the religious tradition of Israel. At key moments in Israel's history, God elects non-Jewish leaders, servants, and laypeople for the Lord to provide wise counsel, theological instruction, exemplary behavior, and correction to the nation of Israel, and later the church. The Bible is full of theological revelation revealed from the outside in, as Gentiles such as Abimelech, Hagar, Zipporah, Jethro, Rahab, Ruth, the Queen of Sheba, the Magi, Pilate's wife, and Cornelius declare God's truth to God's people. This biblical motif continues in our present-day contexts as the Lord works from outside the boundaries of God's people. Those outside the Jewish and Christian traditions may thus become active participants in the mission of God, the *missio Dei*, in which the Lord desires to draw all peoples, including Israel and the church, into the kingdom.

---

[34] Bruce, *The Book of Acts*, 202.

Conclusion

Robert L. Gallagher

The conclusion of our book first includes a summary of the chapter content that we presented: a biblical and contemporary exploration of the fulfillment of God's mission through Gentiles. Following this synopsis is a missiological-theological analysis of a number of themes in the manuscript describing their significance for understanding God's universal mission to and through the nations. Next, we undertake a conversation about the importance of the project for contemporary debates on global mission in religion and society. Then we discuss future topics of study before our concluding section.

Breaking Through the Boundaries: Biblical Perspectives on Mission from the Outside In sets forth the biblical narrative of God's mission as fulfilled by those outside of Jewish purview. In other words, the project covered a biblical and current survey of the *missio Dei* from the outside in, which shows the Lord's inclusion of Gentiles as missionaries to God's people. The volume introduces the concept of God working beyond human boundaries from a scriptural and socio-historiographic perspective. Salvation history constantly demonstrates that God instructs the Lord's people through persons who are outside the religious tradition of Israel and the church. The scriptures are full of divine insights exposed from the outside in. For example, Gentiles such as Hagar, Jethro, the Magi, Ruth, and Cornelius declare God's truth to God's people.

PRESENTATION SUMMARY

We covered a great deal of ground in this book: from Abraham in Genesis to Cornelius in Acts. Our analysis ranged geographically from Canaanite territory and the Midian desert to Susa (the capital of the Persian Empire) and Caesarea (the Roman center of first-century Palestine). In addition, the review considered Gentiles: three men and four women, together with five groups of males, all of whom were of a variety of ethnicities and occupations (2000 BCE to 50 CE). The participants included a Babylonian businessman, a female Egyptian slave, a Midianite king and princess, a peasant Moabitess, a number of Philistine clans, a Persian queen, a scientific community from the East, and a Roman soldier.

We now remind the reader of the key missional issues of the book by providing a brief summary of each chapter.

Abraham: Abraham receives God's correction, blessing, and counsel through his Gentile neighbors: an Egyptian pharaoh becomes Abraham's conscience when Abraham lies about Sarah, his wife; Melchizedek, king of Salem, serves as Yahweh's priest, blessing Abraham; and Abimelech, king of Gerar, through a covenantal treaty, becomes Abraham's political ally and counsel. Throughout Abraham's lifetime God uses individuals from outside the covenant community of Israel to serve as the Lord's voice to the patriarch.

Hagar: As an Egyptian, Hagar encountered the God of her Israelite mistress as a religious outsider. During Hagar's interaction with Yahweh, God proclaims a covenantal blessing upon Hagar and her son and physically saves them both from death. In turn, Hagar names this benevolent God "El roi," the "God who sees me" (Gen 16:13). It is through this unique encounter that God's people receive new insight into the nature and character of God. The Lord uses Hagar, a young Gentile woman who Israel socially and religiously marginalizes, to teach God's people about God's unconditional love and grace.

Jethro and Zipporah: When Jethro meets Moses in the wilderness, and Jethro declares that Yahweh is the most powerful sovereign in all the earth, Jethro, as a Gentile, performs the Bible's first recorded ritual of sacrifice to Yahweh. Furthermore, Jethro's daughter Zipporah becomes Moses's wife and migrates with Moses to lead the Hebrews out of Egypt. On the way she circumvents Yahweh's anger by circumcising her son and ushers her entire family into the Hebrew covenant.

Philistine tribes: The case studies of four Philistine tribes migrating from Gath show the intersection of migration and mission. Obed-edom (the keeper of the Ark), the Cherethites and Pelethites (King David's Philistine bodyguard), and Ittai (the Gittite warrior-leader), loyal to David during Absalom's revolt, all migrated to Jerusalem and influenced the evolving destiny of the inhabitants of the holy city and Israel. This study demonstrates that migration plays a role in the mission of God, and that we should consider this movement as a contemporary strategy of mission.

Ruth: The two widows, Naomi and Ruth, in their patriarchal culture, depict a rare and beautiful relationship between a mother-in-law and her migrant daughter-in-law. Facing insurmountable obstacles as widows, the two women creatively find a way to sustain themselves. The book of Ruth offers contemporary readers the wisdom of changing obstacles into vehicles of opportunity.

Esther and Mordecai: Esther and Mordecai are cross-cultural power brokers who migrate to the palace of King Xerxes and befriend the enemy to accomplish their mission of saving God's people from genocide. In this situation they reverse the power of the "other" to save their kinfolks. King Xerxes changes sides and empowers Esther and Mordecai through twists and turns and multiple reversals in his court. Truce and reconciliation, as initiated by Esther and Mordecai, have widespread leadership relevance in a contemporary conflict-ridden and violent world.

The Magi: When the Magi, who migrated from the Persian context of Zoroastrianism, come to Jerusalem to worship the king of the Jews, the gospel writer draws a sharp difference between the disturbed Herod and the Jewish leadership, and the worshipful Magi. The contrast represents the first fruits of Matthew's theme that compares the unbelief of the Jewish leadership to the astounding belief of the Gentiles. The Magi narrative declares the universality of the mission of Jesus. Jesus is not only "king of the Jews" (Mt 2:6) but king of the entire world; this is proclaimed when the believers are sent to make disciples of all nations (Mt 28:16–20).

Peter and Cornelius: Cornelius is a consecrated person outside the sphere of Christian mission activity, to whom God sends an angel to respect his Gentile godliness. Peter comes to his home, at which time the Gentile gathers his family and friends, and the Holy Spirit falls upon them. Peter's engagement becomes a catalyst for Jewish Christians to engage in Gentile mission. Furthermore, the apostle Peter undergoes a transformation as the Gentile demonstrates to the Christian leader an attribute of God of which Peter was not fully aware.

THEMATIC ANALYSIS

In the introduction to *Breaking Through the Boundaries* we examined some missional themes to introduce our volume, such as approaches to interreligious conversation and hospitality as an agent of mission. The following section expands on the subject of hospitality and mission and expounds upon another theme emerging from this book: migration and mission.

Hospitality and Mission

The embracing of hospitality in ministry, or conversely, the deficiency of hospitality, is a significant missional tapestry throughout the scriptures. In Luke 10, the disciples' abhorrence of the Samaritans is inflamed due to the half-Jewish people refusing them hospitality; this curtails any likelihood of loving mission. In contrast to this negative aspect, Simon the tanner hosts Peter at his seaside business-home. Peter in turn gives hospitality to the Gentile servants and soldiers of Cornelius, as well as receiving the table fellowship of the Roman centurion. In Acts 10:41, Peter in his apostolic sermon emphasizes that he and the disciples ate and drank with Jesus after the resurrection. The declaration is significant because it underscores the followers' intimacy with the risen Lord, in conjunction with Jesus's ability to be fully human in his glorified body (see Jesus eating in the upper room [Lk 24:36–43], cooking breakfast on the beach [Jn 21:9–14], and highlighting the importance of meal-communion with Gentiles in the continuing ministry of Jesus and his kingdom [Lk 5:30; 14:23–24]).

Last, eating with Gentiles was a problem for the Jerusalem Christians. "So when Peter went up to Jerusalem, the circumcised believers criticized him and said, 'You went into the house of uncircumcised men and ate with them'" (Acts 11:2–3). Yet they eventually concluded, "So then, even to Gentiles God has granted repentance that leads to life" (Acts 11:18). In the midst of Peter's cross-cultural ministry, these different opportunities of sharing meals with Gentiles laid the foundation of the Holy Spirit's descent upon non-Jewish people and the breaking forth of the Gentile mission. Roots and hints of this theme go all the way back to the early chapters of this volume in which the Gentiles Melchizedek and Jethro serve meals to the Jewish patriarchs Abraham and Moses.

Migration and Mission

Migration is another missional theme evident throughout the chapters of our book. Migration has been important since the day of Pentecost and has shaped Christianity from the early church until the present day. Each of the chapters looked at migration theologically as people moved to and fro throughout the Bible, drawing out principles from these narratives that has an acute relevance to today's churning global migratory patterns. Migration has become extremely important in our contemporary world, as Christians and non-Christians stream into various global contexts from the majority world and beyond. On the one hand, migrants often bring with them political turmoil and financial tensions; on the other, they produce opportunities for hospitality and church revitalization.

In a short time the world has drastically changed, and through migration it is in constant fluctuation. The situation is not going to subside in the near future. Fortunately, the Bible has insights that illumine the challenges of our age, which the church, unfortunately, has not sufficiently addressed. Our book allowed an exploration of migration, which provides answers to a Christian world that finds itself on the move. Our project uncovered a contribution to theology that is encouraging to responsible Christians who desire a way forward.

Throughout the work Gentiles migrating as missionaries to bless God's people is a repeated theme. Abraham, Hagar, Jethro, Zipporah, the four tribes of Philistia, Ruth, Esther and Mordecai, the Magi, and Cornelius all migrated from their original homes. This is reverse mission. It is important to realize, conversely, that we should not confine the definition of *mission* to the concept of mission involving only those who are sent by God. This is not the only form of mission. Any intercultural encounter is a potential missional situation because God communicates in the context of cross-cultural intersections. An intercultural encounter is missional, whatever the motive or reason, and no matter who initiates it.

From *Breaking Through the Boundaries* let us briefly consider three episodes of Gentile migration and God's mission. First, Cornelius, an Italian migrant outside the sphere of Christian mission, engaged with Peter and becomes a catalyst for the early church to engage in Gentile mission. Second, the Midianite Zipporah, who migrates with Moses to Egypt, circumcises her son and incises her family into the Hebrew covenant. Last, the Magi, who migrate from Persia to Jerusalem to worship the king of the Jews, point to the universality of Christ's mission as king of the nations. We could continue to draw out examples from our survey of non-Jewish immigrants whom God uses as cross-cultural change agents, such as Hagar, Ruth, and the Philistine clans loyal to King David.

CONTEMPORARY DEBATES

In our conclusion so far we have considered the content and major ministry themes of the book chapters. We now contemplate two religious and social debates that affect contemporary global mission. Initially, the central thrust of the First and Second Testaments is God's mission. There are rivers of missional tapestries that run throughout the scriptures opposing the nugget hermeneutical approach of sporadically selecting verses that support our biased notions of mission. The whole Bible is full of cross-cultural encounters. We could ask who in the scriptures is involved in intercultural encounters. The list of biblical characters is extensive as God connects person after person with people from cultures other than their own. Perhaps we could rephrase the question: Who in the Bible is *not* involved in intercultural encounters?

Interpretative Blind Spot

Even so, many theological endeavors neglect to view the Bible from a cross-cultural viewpoint. So many theological commentaries fail to appreciate the cultural and/or cross-cultural aspects of the events they are interpreting. Often scholars see the scriptures dimly through their own cultural lens. We believe that this is an interpretative blind spot in Christian scholarship. Blind spots are prominent in church history, and it is imperative that we learn from our historical mistakes. For example, through the centuries the cruelty and injustice of human slavery were biblically justified. In the twenty-first century, looking back at that era, we ask how the church could possibly justify human trafficking. Yet, what are today's blind spots that we do not perceive, which in one hundred years' time the followers of Christ, looking back on our epoch, will ask the same question? For example, how could Christians not see the truth of the suppression of the majority world by Western capitalist greed in food supplies, medical assistance, and disease prevention; the indifference and avarice of national governments and industrial monopolies toward the perils of climate change and the proliferation of military armaments; the unequal global economic distribution between the haves and the have nots; institutionalizing societal problems such as homes for the aged, wards for the dying, prisons, and mental hospitals; the power obsession of the Western church toward majority-world Christianity through theological, financial, and publication dominance; the stifling entwining of Western Christianity and national politics; and the repression by the church of women using their God-given talents in ministerial leadership and mission.

In the succeeding part of this conclusion we consider one of the church's contemporary hermeneutical blind spots that our book begins to address. There is much academic time, energy, and money devoted to a number of current controversies in mission, such as the value of short-term missions, lack of training of entering missionaries, the rich lifestyle of missionaries versus the poor lifestyle of locals, raising up nationals in leadership instead of sending more Western missionaries, controversy of the "insider movements," Arabic translations using familial language in Muslim ministries, how to accomplish missions in a post-Christendom Western context, and the balance between proclamation evangelism in relation to holistic mission, which is still an ongoing digression.

Women as Faithful Leaders

There is one continuing controversy within the church, however, which is still undervalued and shamefully neglected: the issue of women in leadership. Our volume shows that women such as Hagar, Zipporah, Ruth, and Esther are faithful representatives of God's revelation. We support the argument not from a few isolated scriptures, but from the illumination of the significant ministries of these biblical women.

We believe that gender is irrelevant for spiritual authority. The subservient role of women to men, especially in regard to spiritual leadership, is another aspect of fallen culture that God wants to overthrow. Church leadership roles and roles in the home are determined by gifting rather than by gender. God's Spirit distributes leadership gifts, such as prophesying, to women as servants of the Lord. Additionally, the New Testament gift lists in context are completely gender neutral, with the Holy Spirit empowering individuals in such a way as to transcend gender, age, and social status. It remains God's prerogative to give gifts to persons, and the Lord will do so as the Spirit pleases, to women and men alike (see Joel 2:28–32; Acts 2:16–21).

Scriptural examples from both the First and Second Testaments of the meta-roles of women are prayers (Hannah of 1 Samuel, and the women in Acts 1), prophets (Deborah and Anna), women of influence (Ruth and Lydia), missionaries (the servant girl of 1 Kings 5, and the Samaritan woman), and theologians (Miriam and Priscilla). In teasing out the meta-role of women theologians we discover a meta-tapestry in the lives of such females as Hagar (Egyptian slave, Gen 16; 21), Tamar (temple prostitute, Gen 38), Asenath (wife of Joseph, Gen 41), Zipporah (wife of Moses, Ex 4), Rahab (Canaanite prostitute, Josh 2), Deborah (Israelite judge, Judg 5), Hannah (mother of Samuel, 1 Sam 2), the choir of David (1 Sam 18; 21; 29), Abigail (wife of King David, 1 Sam 25), the Israelite wise women (2 Sam 14), Bathsheba (wife of Uriah the Hittite, 1 Kgs 1—2), the Queen of Sheba (1 Kgs 10), the mothers of Israel (Prov 1; 6), Esther (Est), Pilate's wife (Mt 27), Elizabeth (Lk 1), Mary (Lk 1), and the Samaritan woman (Jn 4). God used these women to declare divine truth and manifest faithful leadership, in spite of men embedding them in varying situations of patriarchal authoritarianism.

In addition, throughout the Bible, Gentile women were followers of the Lord in the role of the *didaskalos* (the dispenser of God's authoritative instruction), to bring about God's corrective purpose at crucial turning points in the history of God's people. Non-Jewish women such as Hagar, (Gen 16:1–16; 21:8–21), Zipporah (Ex 4:24–26), Rahab (Josh 2:8–10, 11–13), Ruth (Ruth), Abigail (1 Sam 25:28–29, 30–31), the Queen of Sheba (1 Kgs 10:6–9), Pilate's spouse (Mt 27:19, 24), and the woman beside the Samaritan well (Jn 4:28–29, 39–42), spoke God's truth to teach the Lord's people so that they would realign their longings toward God and fulfill God's missional commitments.

This is the primary evangelical disagreement concerning the current debate over women in leadership: Is it appropriate for women to aspire to leadership roles within the church that will place them in positions of authority over men? Who is asking the question, however? God or men of power? God used Gentile women to teach the nation of Israel—including male leaders—to turn the nation toward God's intentions. Undeniably, God can use women to teach the church—including male leaders—to turn Christ's disciples toward the desires of God.

With this claim in mind, the most appropriate response for today's church is for both men and women to put aside the cloak of power and embrace the towel of servanthood—to plead with God regarding their lives and blind boundaries that the Lord Jesus would patiently massage their souls to remove the calloused bigotry and bring about a falling away of the opinionated barriers in order for them to dispense Yahweh's love and grace in global mission.

FUTURE STUDY

Examination of the preceding list of Gentile and Jewish women of theological grace reveals that of the over twenty women mentioned (in addition to the four women groups), *Breaking Through the Boundaries* only explored four Gentile women (Hagar, Zipporah, Vashti, and Ruth). Similarly, numerous biblical persons need further examination within a missiological framework. Scholars have accomplished little missiological research, not only of the women listed above, but also of Gentiles such as Melchizedek (Gen 14), Abimelech (Gen 21; 22; 26), Balaam (Num 22—24), the inhabitants of Gath (1—2 Sam), the widow of Zarepath (1 Kgs 17), Nebuchadnezzar (Dan 1—4), Darius (Dan 6), Cyrus (Ezr 1—6), and the Samaritan leper (Lk 17). To this research inventory could be added those of the Jewish faith such as Daniel (Dan) with Elijah and Elisha (1—2 Kgs), and Christians such as Titus (Ti), Philemon (Phlm), Timothy (1—2 Tim), and Paul (his epistles), to name only a few. All of these are in cross-cultural situations worthy of missiological exploration.

JESUS THE CROSS-CULTURAL WORKER

Another area of needed study is Jesus as a cross-cultural worker. Very few theologians see Christ ministering as a missionary. The usual theological default is programming Jesus the Jew ministering to the Jewish people in Judea with the restrictions of Matthew 10:5–6 reverberating through the research:. "These twelve Jesus sent out with the following instructions: 'Do not go among the Gentiles or enter any town of the Samaritans. Go rather to the lost sheep of Israel.'" In parentheses, we would add the phrase "at this time," because viewing the wider panorama of Jesus's ministry does not agree with this specific ministry restriction (cf. Mt 28:16–20).

All four Gospels witness the care of the Master toward non-Jewish people. As we have seen in a number of chapters of our work, Luke 7:1–10 records the healing of the Roman centurion's servant who was about to die (cf. Mt 8:5–13). When Jesus heard the humble response of the centurion believing in the Lord's creative word, he marveled and told his Jewish audience, "I tell you, I have not found such great faith even in Israel" (7:9). Complementing the healing of the servant is the deliverance of a woman's daughter from the region of Tyre and Sidon (Mt 15:21–28; cf. Mk 7:24–30). Similar to the non-Jewish soldier, Jesus acknowledges that the Gentile mother had great faith; she is another non-Jewish model of faith toward God for Israel to emulate (Mt 15:28).

The consequences of the early ministry of Jesus was a caravan of people traveling to multicultural Galilee to hear the Lord's teaching and experience his miracles (see Mt 4:15; Isa 9:1; cf. Lk 1:79). The Gospels record great multitudes following him from Galilee, Decapolis, and beyond the Jordan, as well as Idumea, Judea, Jerusalem, and the vicinity of Tyre and Sidon (Mt 4:23–25; Mk 3:7–8; Lk 6:17–19). God's kingdom expansion exposed the first disciples to the Messiah proclaiming the gospel and healing the sick from a diverse array of different cultures and ethnicities.

Equally, there is evidence of Christ going to non-Jewish territory to preach the kingdom of God and heal the sick in Gerasenes (Mk 5:1–20), the Decapolis (Mk 7:31–37), Magadan (Mt 15:39), Tyre (Mk 7:31), Dalmanutha (Mk 8:1), and beyond the Jordan (Mk 10:1). This proves God's borderless love of all nations; Jesus's mission was not limited to homogeneous Jewish Judea and therefore is worthy of further missiological study.

IN CONCLUSION

Henri J. M. Nouwen tells the story of burnout from overly ambitious work and his desperate need for rest and renovation. He thus decided to spend some quiet time in the L'Arche community north of Paris. There he found physically and mentally challenged individuals who did not know him and who were uninterested in his achievements. He reveals, "When these people welcomed me with a deep and sincere affection, a new place within me was opened up. The authentic love of these 'outsiders' broke right through my self-rejection, and gave me a glimpse of a love that was much earlier and more original than I was. It was an experience of the first love. It was the voice calling me the Beloved."[1]

Nouwen's experience is parallel to the biblical theme of *Breaking Through the Boundaries;* that is, God has always worked with the "outsiders" in revealing to the "people of God" aspects of the Lord's character, which could only be achieved using Gentiles as missionaries. There is an opposition, however, to this perception of God at work. We can smother the voice of God through fear of losing power and control of our religious securities due to attitudes of theological superiority.

---

[1] Henri J. M. Nouwen, "Forgiveness: The Name of Love in a Wounded World," *Weavings: Woven Together in Love: A Journal of the Christian Life* 7, no. 2 (1992): 52.

The patriarch Abraham and the apostle Peter eventually understood this quandary. In Genesis 20:11, Abraham finally confesses to Abimelech, king of Gerar, whom he has shamed by his behavior, "I said to myself, 'There is surely no fear of God in this place.'" Abraham's religious presumption was incorrect. Peter, after twenty years of God's dealings, also came to the same conclusion as the father of our faith when he states before Gentile Cornelius, "I now realize how true it is that God does not show favoritism, but accepts from every nation the one who fears him and does what is right" (Acts 10:34–35). Both Peter and Abraham feared losing theological control, which blinded them to seeing the fear or reverence of God resident in the Gentiles whom the Lord brought across their path.

Parker J. Palmer summarizes the key issue: "God uses the stranger to shake us from our conventional points of view, to remove the scales of worldly assumptions from our eyes. God is a stranger to us, and it is at the risk of missing God's truth that we domesticate God, reduce God to the role of familiar friend."[2] The concept endures in our current global contexts as God continues to work from outside the boundaries of God's people. Gentiles thus become active participants in the mission of God, the *missio Dei*, in which the sovereign God desires

> a great multitude that no one could count, from every nation, tribe, people and language, standing before the throne and before the Lamb. They were wearing white robes and were holding palm branches in their hands. And they cried out in a loud voice:
>
> > "Salvation belongs to our God,
> > who sits on the throne,
> > and to the Lamb." (Rev 7:9–10)

---

[2] Parker J. Palmer, *The Company of Strangers* (New York: Crossroad, 1994), 59.

Author Biographies

Paul Hertig, PhD, professor of global studies at Azusa Pacific University, has integrated biblical and intercultural studies throughout his teaching career. He has published over twenty essays along with the following books: *Matthew's Narrative Use of Galilee in the Multicultural and Missiological Journeys of Jesus*; *Mission in Acts: Ancient Narratives in Contemporary Context*; *Landmark Essays in Mission and World Christianity*; and *Contemporary Mission Theology: Engaging the Nations*—the latter three books co-edited with Robert L. Gallagher.

Young Lee Hertig, PhD, co-founder and executive director of ISAAC (Innovative Space for Asian American Christianity) and AAWOL (Asian American Women on Leadership) in Los Angeles, California, is a senior lecturer at Azusa Pacific University and former associate professor at United Theological Seminary and assistant professor at Fuller Theological Seminary. She has published widely on spirituality, sustainability, and diversity from a yinist intersectional perspective, having coined the term *yinist* in engagement with feminist, womanist, and *mujerista* discourses. She holds three MAs—in counseling psychology, theology, and anthropology—and the PhD in intercultural studies (Fuller Theological Seminary).

Sarita Gallagher Edwards, PhD, is an associate professor of religion at George Fox University in Newberg, Oregon. Sarita served as a missionary with CRC Churches International in Papua New Guinea and Australia, and she teaches in the areas of biblical theology, intercultural studies, world religions, and world Christianity. Her publications include *Abrahamic Blessing: A Missiological Narrative of Revival in Papua New Guinea.*

Robert L. Gallagher, PhD, is the director and a professor of intercultural studies at Wheaton College Graduate School in Chicago, where he has taught since 1998. He previously served as the president of the American Society of Missiology (2010–11). His publications include the following books co-edited with Paul Hertig: *Mission in Acts: Ancient Narratives in Contemporary Context*; *Landmark Essays in Mission and World Christianity*; and *Contemporary Mission Theology: Engaging the Nations.* He is co-author, with John Mark Terry, of *Encountering the History of Missions: From the Early Church to Today.*

The American Society of Missiology Series

1. *Protestant Pioneers in Korea*, Everett Nichols Hunt, Jr.
2. *Catholic Politics in China and Korea*, Eric O. Hanson
3. *From the Rising of the Sun: Christians and Society in Contemporary Japan*, James M. Phillips
4. *Meaning across Cultures*, Eugene A. Nida and William D. Reyburn
5. *The Island Churches of the Pacific*, Charles W. Forman
6. *Henry Venn: Missionary Statesman*, Wilbert R. Shenk
7. *No Other Name? Christianity and Other World Religions*, Paul F. Knitter
8. *Toward a New Age in Christian Theology*, Richard Henry Drummond
9. *The Expectation of the Poor: Latin American Base Ecclesial Communities in Protest*, Guillermo Cook
10. *Eastern Orthodox Mission Theology Today*, James J. Stamoolis
11. *Confucius, the Buddha, and Christ: A History of the Gospel in China*, Ralph R. Covell
12. *The Church and Cultures: New Perspectives in Missiological Anthropology*, Louis J. Luzbetak, SVD
13. *Translating the Message: The Missionary Impact on Culture*, Lamin Sanneh
14. *An African Tree of Life*, Thomas G. Christensen
15. *Missions and Money: Affluence as a Western Missionary Problem . . . Revisited* (second edition), Jonathan J. Bonk
16. *Transforming Mission: Paradigm Shifts in Theology of Mission*, David J. Bosch
17. *Bread for the Journey: The Mission and Transformation of Mission*, Anthony J. Gittins, C.S.Sp.
18. *New Face of the Church in Latin America: Between Tradition and Change*, edited by Guillermo Cook

19. *Mission Legacies: Biographical Studies of Leaders of the Modern Missionary Movement,* edited by Gerald H. Anderson, Robert T. Coote, Norman A. Horner, and James M. Phillips

20. *Classic Texts in Mission and World Christianity,* edited by Norman E. Thomas

21. *Christian Mission: A Case Study Approach,* Alan Neely

22. *Understanding Spiritual Power: A Forgotten Dimension of Cross-Cultural Mission and Ministry,* Marguerite G. Kraft

23. *Missiological Education for the 21st Century: The Book, the Circle, and the Sandals,* edited by J. Dudley Woodberry, Charles Van Engen, and Edgar J. Elliston

24. *Dictionary of Mission: Theology, History, Perspectives,* edited by Karl Müller, SVD, Theo Sundermeier, Stephen B. Bevans, SVD, and Richard H. Bliese

25. *Earthen Vessels and Transcendent Power: American Presbyterians in China, 1837–1952,* G. Thompson Brown

26. *The Missionary Movement in American Catholic History,* Angelyn Dries, OSF

27. *Mission in the New Testament: An Evangelical Approach,* edited by William J. Larkin Jr. and Joel W. Williams

28. *Changing Frontiers of Mission,* Wilbert R. Shenk

29. *In the Light of the Word: Divine Word Missionaries of North America,* Ernest Brandewie

30. *Constants in Context: A Theology of Mission for Today,* Stephen B. Bevans, SVD, and Roger P. Schroeder, SVD

31. *Changing Tides: Latin America and World Mission Today,* Samuel Escobar

32. *Gospel Bearers, Gender Barriers: Missionary Women in the Twentieth Century,* edited by Dana L. Robert

33. *Church: Community for the Kingdom,* John Fuellenbach, SVD

34. *Mission in Acts: Ancient Narratives in Contemporary Context,* edited by Robert L. Gallagher and Paul Hertig

35. *A History of Christianity in Asia: Volume I, Beginnings to 1500,* Samuel Hugh Moffett

36. *A History of Christianity in Asia: Volume II, 1500–1900*, Samuel Hugh Moffett

37. *A Reader's Guide to Transforming Mission*, Stan Nussbaum

38. *The Evangelization of Slaves and Catholic Origins in Eastern Africa*, Paul V. Kollman, CSC

39. *Israel and the Nations: A Mission Theology of the Old Testament*, James Chukwuma Okoye, C.S.Sp.

40. *Women in Mission: From the New Testament to Today*, Susan E. Smith

41. *Reconstructing Christianity in China: K. H. Ting and the Chinese Church*, Philip L. Wickeri

42. *Translating the Message: The Missionary Impact on Culture* (second edition), Lamin Sanneh

43. *Landmark Essays in Mission and World Christianity*, edited by Robert L. Gallagher and Paul Hertig

44. *World Mission in the Wesleyan Spirit*, Darrell L. Whiteman and Gerald H. Anderson (published by Province House, Franklin, TN)

45. *Miracles, Missions, & American Pentecostalism*, Gary B. McGee

46. *The Gospel among the Nations: A Documentary History of Inculturation*, Robert A. Hunt

47. *Missions and Unity: Lessons from History, 1792–2010*, Norman E. Thomas (published by Wipf and Stock, Eugene, OR)

48. *Mission and Culture: The Louis J. Luzbetak Lectures*, edited by Stephen B. Bevans

49. *Comprehending Mission: The Questions, Methods, Themes, Problems, and Prospects of Missiology*, Stanley H. Skreslet

50. *Christian Mission among the Peoples of Asia*, Jonathan Y. Tan

51. *Sent Forth: African Missionary Work in the West*, Harvey C. Kwiyani

52. *Mangoes or Bananas: The Quest for an Authentic Asian Christian Theology*, Hwa Yung

53. *Contemporary Mission Theology: Engaging the Nations: Essays in Honor of Charles E. Van Engen*, edited by Robert L. Gallagher and Paul Hertig

54. *African Christian Leadership: Realities, Opportunities, and Impact*, edited by Kirimi Barine and Robert Priest

55. *Women Leaders in the Student Christian Movement: 1880–1920*, Thomas Russell

56. *Traditional Ritual as Christian Worship: Dangerous Syncretism or Necessary Hybridity?*, edited by R. Daniel Shaw and William R. Burrows

57. *Christian Mission, Contextual Theology, Prophetic Dialogue: Essays in Honor of Stephen B. Bevans, SVD*, edited by Dale T. Irvin and Peter C. Phan

58. *Go Forth: Toward a Community of Missionary Disciples*, Pope Francis, selected with commentary by William P. Gregory

59. *Breaking Through the Boundaries: Biblical Perspectives on Mission from the Outside In*, Paul Hertig, Young Lee Hertig, Sarita Gallagher Edwards, and Robert L. Gallagher